Saints' Names for Your Baby

Saints' Names for Your Baby

Fiona MacMath

A Liturgical Press Book

THE LITURGICAL PRESS
Collegeville, Minnesota

Cover design by Ann Blattner. Photos © 1999 Penny Gentieu.

The Scripture quotations contained herein are from the New Revised Standard Version Bible, Catholic edition, © 1989 by the Division of Christian Education of the National Council of Churches of Christ in the USA. Used by permission. All rights reserved.

First published in Great Britain in 1997 by Marshall Pickering, an imprint of HarperCollins*Publishers* under the title *Saints' Names for Your Baby.*

© 1997 Fiona MacMath

The text of The Liturgical Press edition of this book has been adapted from the original by Nancy McDarby.

Published in the United States of America and in Canada by The Liturgical Press, Collegeville, MN 56321.

1	2	3	4	5	6	7	8	9

Library of Congress Cataloging-in-Publication Data

MacMath, Fiona.
    Saints' names for your baby / Fiona MacMath.
        p.   cm.
    ISBN 0-8146-2703-X (alk. paper)
    1. Christian saints Dictionaries. 2. Names, Personal
Dictionaries.   I. Title.
    BR1710.M24   2000
    270'.092'.2—dc21   99-16137
    [B]   CIP

Dedicated to
Elizabeth Anne Vinten Pinner

Introduction

Our babies come into the world as surprise parcels, each with a unique bundle of characteristics. We have to wait to see them gradually unfold but cannot wait until then, though, to give them names; so we choose a name in the hope that they will grow into it and like it. We choose names because they sound well, because they belong to someone we love, or because they mean something important to us.

For centuries, people have bestowed a saint's name on their baby in the hope that their child will grow up like its namesake, even though many of the saints were notoriously difficult to live with! The saints are also believed to offer a range of services to their protégés: protection, of course, help for specific problems, such as the rigors of traveling, and help for special talents, like music or resourcefulness. For example, a child called Clare—named after St. Francis's prayerful companion—might be able to draw on the single-mindedness, charity, and kindness of her namesake. More prosaically, she is the patron saint of television: her name means "light." (Ironically, she is also invoked to help sore eyes.)

Some ideas for a future career, perhaps? St. George might point to a profession in the armed forces. St. Cecilia could give your budding musician an unfair advantage over everyone else. St. Anne might have a child dedicated to her if she had helped with a difficult birth; and St. Giles is traditionally the special saint of anyone born with a handicap of some sort.

To bear the name of a saint certainly means having something to live up to—or even to live down. It would be a very unkind parent who christened their child Ethelburga or Willibald. But to have a "heavenly" godmother or godfather is to be part of the tradition of the Church, to have a name which is familiar throughout the Christian world. It is to have a star to follow.

How, then, do you choose a saint's name for your baby? In medieval times, people seem to have been led more by devotion to certain popular saints than conventional ideas about what girls or boys should be called—many girls were christened in honor of male saints, with what we would think of nowadays as exclusively boys' names. Since the church's calendar remembers several saints on any given day in the year, babies were often christened hastily by a priest after the saint's feast day on which they were born. Since some Christians (particularly Roman Catholics and Orthodox) celebrate a person's "name day" even more splendidly than his or her birthday, it might be an advantage to choose a saint whose feast day is a good way off from the actual birthday—and thus have two celebrations every year.

If you are not familiar with the way Christians have venerated the saints, you may be rather surprised by what you read. Some appear to be mythological, some seem to be characters in legends. Others seem to have been canonized simply because they died in a horrible way or because they have a dubious reputation for weird phenomena like levitation or miraculous healing. The veneration of so many women for choosing death rather than marriage is at odds with our own century's veneration of sexual fulfillment and it may now seem rather pointless. But it is faith and love that matter, and no one without these—however spiritually powerful or gruesomely killed—can be called a saint.

Where there is little information available about a particular saint, perhaps the faith and love of the people who have been inspired by him or her is of the most importance. It is a kind of devotion to God through a human character who is more recognizably like ourselves or closer to our own culture than Jesus is—and he does not despise our need to see him in human form.

This book will give you an idea of some traditional saints' names which are popular today, with something about their first owners—their characters, their special interests, and their dates, where they are known. It may surprise you to see how many variations there are on some names. For instance, Ewan, Siobhan, Joan, Janine, Owen, and Jack are all variations on the name of John. Each entry has variations associated with boys or girls, although these distinctions have never been hard and fast. At the end of the book, there is a calendar of saints, which contains names for every day of the year. The calendars of Christian churches differ, and are changed slightly from time to time, so you may want to do further research yourself if you have a favorite saint.

St. Adrian

Meaning: "from Adria," a port on the Adriatic Sea

Male variation: Adrien

Female variations: Adrianne, Adrienne

This name became widely known in England in the twelfth century, when Nicholas Breakespear took it on becoming the first and only English pope—Adrian IV. It was actually St. Adrian III, however, who was canonized, although no one knows much about his life. An earlier Adrian, and his companion Eubulus, were martyred in Caesarea in 309 for visiting the Christians in prison there, and there was a St. Adrian martyred by the Danes on one of their raids on the Scottish coasts in the ninth century. Another St. Adrian was an African who became the abbot of Canterbury, where he died peacefully in 710.

The most well-known St. Adrian, married to St. Natalia, was also martyred, in 304, for looking after persecuted Christians. He was a Roman soldier in Nicomedia who was so impressed by his Christian prisoners that he joined them. His wife encouraged him in his quest for martyrdom, and is herself venerated as a martyr, although she fled to Agyropolis after his execution, where she died of natural causes.

Feast day: August 26

Symbols: armor; a hammer and anvil; a key; a wheel

Patron: of arms dealers, butchers, and prison officers

St. Agnes

Meaning: **from the Greek, "pure"**

Variations: Agneta, Annis, Ines, Inez, Nessie, Nesta, Senga

St. Agnes (whose name sounds like the Latin *agnus* or "lamb") was reputedly the daughter of a wealthy Christian Roman family during the reign of the emperor Diocletian (284–305), when Christians were savagely persecuted. She is remembered for her determination to remain a virgin, in spite of all the entreaties and threats of Eutropius, the son of a Roman governor, who had fallen in love with her. She was humiliated and threatened with rape by Eutropius, who—legend has it—was immediately struck blind and then miraculously cured by Agnes herself. Eventually, she was sentenced to be burnt at the stake, but the fire seemed more inclined to burn the spectators than her, so she was eventually stabbed to death in 304 or 305. She was only 13 years old. She is one of the few women saints who are mentioned in the liturgy of the Roman Catholic Mass.

"To play the Agnes" is a French expression to describe a young girl who is completely innocent of any idea of love, and Molière includes her as a character in his play *L'école des femmes.* In Britain, however, St. Agnes' Eve was the time when a young girl might be granted a vision of her future husband if she fasted and observed certain rituals before going to bed. Aubrey's *Miscellany* suggests:

> *Upon St. Agnes' night, you take a row of pins and pull out every one, one after another. Saying a paternoster, stick a pin in your sleeve, and you will dream of him or her you shall marry.*

Alternatively, you could fast all day and then eat an egg with salt just before going to bed, or sit up late at your mirror in the hope of catching a glimpse of his face appearing over your shoulder. . . .

Feast day: January 21

Symbols: a lamb; a dove holding a ring; a sword

Patron: of young girls, virgins, and Girl Guides

St. Albert

Meaning: **from Old German, "noble bright"**

Male variations: Aubert, Bertie, Bert

Female variation: Alberta

The name Albert has fallen out of favor after its immense popularity with the Victorians—perhaps it is due for a revival. There are at least seven saints who bear the name, but two are particularly inspiring for us today.

The first, Albert the Great, a German, became one of the most advanced scientists of his age (the thirteenth century). He resigned his bishopric in Regensburg and devoted himself to writing books on logic and mathematics, astronomy and geography, physics and chemistry, the natural sciences and philosophy, as well as theology and ethics. It was under his influence that Thomas Aquinas was encouraged to develop his own systematic theology based on scientific methods.

Feast day: November 15

Patron: of all those involved in scientific and medical research

Another St. Albert, Albert Chmielkowski, was a Polish painter who lost a leg in an uprising against the Russians in 1863, when he was only 18 years old. He later joined the Third Order of the Franciscans (for lay men and women), and made his studio into a shelter for the poor and homeless, before becoming a tramp himself; he died in a hospice in Krakow on Christmas Day, 1916. He might be the inspiration for the "Crisis at Christmas movement," now simply called "Crisis"—an organization which helps the destitute all year round.

Feast Day: December 25

St. Alexander

Meaning: **from the Greek, "defender of men"**

Male variations: Alec, Alex, Alastair, Alisdair, Alexis, Sandy, Sacha

Female variations: Alexandra, Alex, Alexis, Alexei, Alessandra, Sandy, Sandie, Sandra, Alla, Zandra, Sasha

St. Alexander of the Sleepless Ones may be an unwelcome but apt name for a baby. This Alexander was a fifth-century army officer in Constantinople. He was prompted to resign his commission and become a monk by the words of Jesus: "If you wish to be perfect, go, sell your possessions, and give the money to the poor, and you will have treasure in heaven; then come, follow me" (Matt 19:21). Stories about his holiness and miracle working were written down by one of his monks in Greek. The "sleepless ones" were 300 monks who settled with him near Constantinople. Alexander divided them into six choirs to sing the Divine Office in turn—day and night— so that they could be praising God ceaselessly and watching faithfully for the return of Christ.

Feast day: January 15

St. Alice

Meaning: **from Old German, "nobility"**

Variations: Alison, Allison, Alicia, Alyssa, Alisa, Adelaide, Aleydis, Alys

St. Alice was a twelfth-century Cistercian nun from Brussels, who contracted leprosy. It was an immense tragedy for her because she had to accept solitary confinement and was unable to drink the consecrated wine from the chalice. Her life and faith, sustained by visions, was described by a member of her community and Alice was canonized for her patience in suffering.

Feast day: June 15

St. Andrew

Meaning: **from the Greek, "manly"**

Male variations: Andreas, Anders, Andy, Drew, André

Female variations: Andrea, Andrée

There have been many Andrews who have been canonized or beatified, but all take their name, of course, from the first disciple of Jesus. Andrew was a fisherman who was called from his nets to become a fisher of people, bringing with him Peter, his brother. Even though he was Peter's brother, he did not become one of Jesus' closest disciples, as did Peter and Zebedee's sons, James and John. Like most of the apostles, the legends about his life after the crucifixion are very colorful and most improbable. It is thought, however, that he also was crucified, on an x-shaped cross, in Patras, Achaia (Greece).

According to legend, Saints Rule and Theneva later took Andrew's bones to Scotland, obeying the voice of an angel which told them to take his relics "to the ends of the earth." Apparently, this revived Andrew; all three built St. Andrew's church, and he became Scotland's patron saint as well as the patron of Russia and Greece.

Feast day: November 30

Symbols: an x-shaped cross; two fishes; a fish hook; fishing nets

Patron: of fishers, sailors, single women, and those with gout

St. Angel

Meaning: from the Greek, "messenger"

Variation: Angelo

The name "Angel" is rare in English-speaking countries, despite Thomas Hardy's use of it in his novel *Tess of the D'Urbevilles.* Yet it is common in Italy where several Angelos were beatified, and where St. Angelo, a Sicilian Carmelite, was murdered in 1220.

Feast day: May 5

Symbols: red and white roses; lilies; three crowns; a book

St. Angela

Variations: Angelica, Angelina, Angeline, Angéle

Much more common than Angel is its female form, Angela. The Blessed Angela of Foligno was a woman of prayer and mysticism. She was an ordinary thirteenth-century Italian wife and mother until she underwent a sudden conversion and joined the Third Order of the Franciscans. This was an order of "tertiaries"—men and women who could not, for various reasons, go into a friary or convent but who wished to live in the world according to the evangelical counsels of poverty, chastity, and obedience. After her husband died, she was able to give away her wealth and attracted to the Third Order a large number of other people who were impressed by her depth of prayer. Her confessor wrote down her account of some of her mystical experiences, and she is remembered on January 4.

St. Angela Merici was the foundress of the Ursuline order (named after St. Ursula)—the first teaching order for women. She was born in Italy in 1474 and orphaned at 15. She became a Franciscan tertiary and became increasingly aware of the poverty of her native town, Desenzano. Determined to do something to help, she began to teach the poorest children, helped by some other women tertiaries. This practice later developed into a community of women who shared a common rule of life and devoted themselves to teaching and caring for young women and children. It was not an easy vocation—women were expected to live in enclosed communities, in traditional orders, wear habits, and take their inspiration from men. Eventually, after her death, Angela's women were forced to conform to a more traditional order. Nevertheless, her vision was important for the development of nursing, education, and the independence of Christian women.

Feast day: January 27

Patron: of universities and women

St. Anne

Meaning: **from the Hebrew, "gracious"**

Variations: Anna, Annette, Anette, Anita, Anya, Annie, Hannah, Nan, Nana, Nancy, Nita

It might be said that if St. Anne had not existed, Christianity would have had to invent her—so important are grandmothers in the natural order of life. St. Anne was the grandmother of Jesus, at least according to the apocryphal Protoevangelion of St. James. Although nothing certain is known about her life, she can be seen—together with Mary and Jesus—in numerous Renaissance paintings. The account of Anna and her husband Joachim's miraculous conception of Mary may be strongly related to the Hebrew story of Hannah's conception of Samuel; in the same way, Mary's song—the Magnificat—echoes Hannah's song of triumphant joy. The mystery of Mary's conception has become known and honored by many Christians, especially Roman Catholics, as the Immaculate Conception.

Feast day: July 26

Symbols: an angel; a flowering rod; a crown; a nest of young birds; Mary in a cradle

Patron: of housewives and grandmothers, pregnant women, cabinet makers, and Canada

St. Anthony

Meaning: **possibly "beyond price" (Latin—one of the patrician Roman families)**

Male variations: Anton, Antoine, Antonio, Tony

Female variations: Antonia, Antoinette, Antonella, Netta, Nettie, Netty, Toni, Tonia, Tonie, Tony

There are two famous St. Anthonys in the church. The first, Anthony the Great, is often known as the "father of monasticism," for it was he who gathered together many of the fourth-century hermits who had fled from worldly distractions into the desert. These first Desert Fathers and Mothers were famous for their lives of severe self-denial and prayer; St. Athanasius' biography of Anthony, however, shows him to have been a wise and moderate man, even though he suffered terrifying temptations through visions. He is supposed to have died around 365 at the age of 105. The smallest pig in a litter and the smallest bell in a carillon are often called the "tantony," thus they have become his symbols: the little pig for the mortal flesh he conquered and the bell as the traditional symbol of hermits.

Feast day: January 17

Symbols: a pig; a goat; two lions; a Tau cross (T); a bell

Patron: of basket and brush makers (the first occupation of the Desert Fathers and Mothers), butchers, grave diggers, and pigs; he is often invoked by eczema sufferers

The second very well-loved St. Anthony was Portuguese (1195–1231), a Franciscan friar born in Lisbon, although he is known as St. Anthony of Padua, where he is buried. His reputation for finding lost things is based on a story that a novice once "borrowed" his prayer book; Anthony prayed for its recovery and the novice returned it after finding himself tormented by a terrible vision.

Anthony's life's work was not finding lost objects, but rather being "the hammer of the heretics"—having been commissioned in a vision by Francis himself to go and preach, mainly in Italy and France. A tale is told that Anthony shamed the people of Rimini, who would not listen to him, by preaching to the fish in the river, causing them to stand on their tails and listen devoutly. Although he is often pictured as a gentle man, with the Christ-child and a lily, Anthony should not be thought of as anyone but a man of great intelligence and energy, full of the Franciscan passion for helping the poor.

Feast day: June 13

Symbols: the Christ-child on a book; lilies; fishes; a chest with a heart

Patron: of the poor, unmarried women, and Portugal; also invoked for good harvests and by those looking for lost property

St. Audrey

Meaning: **from Old English, "noble strength"**

Variation: Etheldreda

The word "tawdry" developed as a name for the sort of gaudy rubbish sold at the great St. Audrey's Fair at Ely, Cambridgeshire, on her feast day, and Shakespeare uses "Audrey" as the name of his irrepressibly lumpen country wench in *As You Like It.* The original Audrey, however, was the beautiful and determined princess

Etheldreda; she seems to have lived up to her name. She was born in a village outside Newmarket in about 630 and took a vow of celibacy which she upheld, even when—for reasons of state—she was twice married. The bishop, St. Wilfrid, supported her resolution, and she eventually founded the abbey of Ely, one of the great double monasteries of the period, in 672. It was famous for its austerity and prayer under her rule, which lasted until 679, when she died of a tumor on her neck.

Feast day: June 23

Symbols: a sunflower; an open money chest

Patron: of those with diseases of the throat and neck, and of Ely

B

St. Barbara

Meaning: **from the Greek, "a foreigner"**

Variations: Bab, Babette, Barbie, Varina

No one knows if, when, or where Barbara really existed. The legend—a seventh-century romance—tells of a beautiful girl who was imprisoned in a tower by her own father, Dioscurus, in order to keep men—especially Christian men—away. But a doctor managed to get into the tower to teach her about the Christian faith, which she immediately accepted—much to her father's fury. Although Barbara survived the torture of the authorities, her father cut off her head, upon which he was struck by lightning and completely incinerated. Whether true or simply a legend, Barbara became a well-loved patron, particularly by those who worked with explosives or those in need of help during thunderstorms. She is no longer in the Roman Martyrology, but there are other Barbaras, for instance, St. Barbara Yi, who feast is May 27.

St. Barnabas

Meaning: **from the Hebrew, "son of consolation"**

Variations: Barnaby, Barney

Although Barnabas was not one of the Twelve, he is called an "apostle"—that is, "one who is sent." Barnabas worked tirelessly to bring the gospel to the people of the Roman Empire; indeed, his first mission was to be a companion to the newly-converted Paul (also called an apostle) when many Christians in Jerusalem could only remember him as the raging persecutor Saul, who witnessed the stoning of St. Stephen. We know from Acts that Barnabas was a Cypriot Jew, "a good man, full of the Holy Spirit and of faith." He accompanied Paul on his first missionary journey and is honored as the founder of the church on Cyprus.

Barnabas was also the cousin of John Mark, the young man who may have written the first Gospel. John Mark started out on the mission with them but disgraced himself—in Paul's eyes, at least—by wearying of the dangers. Barnabas, to his everlasting credit, took the part of the younger man and went back with him although later he managed to reconcile the two. The Bible does not tell us what became of Barnabas although tradition says that he was martyred at Salamis, Greece. Since Barnabas' feast day is June 11 (the old style Midsummer Day), he has become the patron saint of haymakers and harvesters as well as of Cyprus.

Feast day: June 11

Symbols: a dalmatic (the special vestment worn by a deacon at Mass); three stones; a hatchet

Patron: of harvesters and Cyprus

St. Bartholomew

Meaning: "son of Tolmai"; possibly from the Hebrew, "son of a farmer"

Male variations: Bart, Bartelmy, Tolly

Female variation: Bartholomea

The original Bartholomew was one of the 12 disciples, possibly even the Nathaniel mentioned in John's Gospel, but nothing definite is known about him. It is said that he took the gospel to Armenia, where he was martyred by being flayed alive. His name was given to several Italian saints and also to Bartholomew of Farne, a Yorkshireman. This Bartholomew was ordained in Norway but returned to Britain and spent 42 years on Farne until his death in 1193. His feast day is on June 24. It is also worth mentioning the remarkable Italian nun, Bartholomea Capitanio, who founded the Sisters of Charity of Lovere in Lombardy, with Vincentia Gerosa. Bartholomea wrote several books on the spiritual life and is still remembered as a strong and unselfish woman. She died at the age of 26. Her feast day is on July 26.

Feast day: August 24

Symbols: a scimitar; three knives; the devil under his feet; St. Matthew's Gospel

Patron: of Armenia, cheese merchants, and tanners

St. Benedict

Meaning: **from the Latin, "blessed"**

Male variations: Ben, Bendix, Benedick, Benet, Bennett, Benito, Bennie, Benny

Female variations: Benedicta, Benita, Bennie, Benny, Binnie

As St. Anthony the Great is known as the "father of monasticism" as a whole, St. Benedict (480–c.550) is the father of that particular form we know so well in the West—embodied in the Benedictine Rule, still hugely influential in the church today. Monastics live, work, and pray in monasteries, while keeping alive the tradition of learning, the arts, and hospitality. Benedict was an Italian born to aristocratic parents and had a twin sister who was also canonized as St. Scholastica. His own monastery was founded at Monte Cassino in 547. Apart from his wisdom and moderation, Benedict was also known as a great healer and one through whom God would raise the dead.

Feast day: July 11

Symbols: a ball of fire, a raven, and a pitcher; briars and roses; a broken cup with a serpent on a book; a monastery on a mountain

Patron: of architects, farm workers, monastics, and Europe

St. Bernard

Meaning: **from Old German, "strong as a bear"**

Variations: Barnard, Barnet, Barney, Bern, Bernhard, Bernie, Berny

Most people think of those splendid, long-haired mountain rescue dogs when they think of St. Bernard, and these were named after St. Bernard of Montjoux (996–1081); his feast day is on May 28, and he is—predictably enough—patron saint of skiers and mountaineers. He was known for his pastoral care of the people of the Alpine valleys of Aosta, Italy, and he set up two hospices for travelers on the passes which now bear his name.

The more ecclesiastically distinguished St. Bernard of Clairvaux was born about 10 years afterwards and became a founder of 68 Cistercian monasteries, as well as playing a part in politics and church councils. He wrote so beautifully that he became known as "Doctor Mellifluous" or "the honey-sweet Doctor."

Feast day: August 20

Symbols: a beehive; a pen and ink; a chained devil

Patron: of beekeepers, honey, and candle makers

St. Bernadette

Variations: Berna, Bernardine, Bernarda, Bernarde, Berneta, Bernie, Berny, Bernice

There have been many other canonized Bernards and Bernardinos, but the best loved of their namesakes must be Bernadette Soubirous, the young shepherd girl who saw visions of Mary at Lourdes. Despite all the fuss which ensued, Bernadette never sought publicity for herself and lived out her short life in a convent at Nevers.

Feast day: April 16

Patron: of shepherds

St. Brigid

Meaning: from Old Irish, "strong"

Variations: Bedelia, Biddy, Birgitta, Bride, Brigitte, Britt, Gita

Brigid, born in Ireland about 450, became so beloved for her charity and her miracle-working powers that it is hard to piece together any factual account of her life. Nevertheless, she was born near Dundalk and founded a monastery at Kildare before her death in 525. *The Book of Lismore* says of her, "Everything that Brigid would ask of the Lord was granted at once, for this was her desire: to satisfy the poor, to drive out every hardship, to spare every miserable man. . . . She is the Mary of Gael." Whether or not she hung her cloak on an obliging sunbeam, as the legend goes, is open to doubt, but that—and not the names and the dates—is what sticks so delightfully in the imagination.

Feast day: February 1

Symbols: a column of fire; a goose; a branch growing from an altar; a cow; a large bowl; wheat; a book

Patron: of dairymaids and poultry women, nuns, Ireland, and New Zealand

St. Bridget

Bridget, born in Sweden nearly 1000 years later than Brigid, could not have had a more different life. She was born into a wealthy family; her marriage produced eight children, one of whom (Katherine of Vadstena) was also to be canonized. She had a place at court and, after she was widowed, became a mystic and writer whose advice was accepted by kings and popes. She founded the Bridgettine Order for men and women at Vadstena, Sweden, but then left the country to travel on pilgrimage. Eventually, she settled in Rome, where she worked among the poor. She died there in 1373.

Feast day: July 23

Patron: of scholars and Sweden

St. Bruno

Meaning: from Old German, "brown"

St. Bruno the Great, son of St. Matilda, was archbishop of Cologne in 953, and a ruler of considerable power in the absence of his brother, the German emperor Otto I.

It is St. Bruno of Chartreuse (born in Cologne in 1030 and named after the archbishop), however, who is much better known, for it was he who founded the great Carthusian monastery of La Grande Chartreuse. Bruno and six others lived much like the first Desert Fathers, in solitude and great poverty. Like his namesake, however, St. Bruno was also called to public life—in this case as papal advisor to Urban II—and he was never allowed to return to his monastery. He died in 1101 in another monastery he founded, called La Torre, in Calabria, Italy.

Feast day: October 11

Symbols: a flowering crucifix; a death's head; a star on his chest; seven stars

Patron: of those who are victims of demonic possession

C

St. Catherine

Meaning: from the Greek, "pure," "clean"

Variations: Catharine, Caitlin, Cathy, Catriona, Cathryn, Cathleen, Caterina, Katherine, Kathryn, Karen, Kate, Kathleen, Katia, Katie, Katy, Kaye, Kit, Kitty, Trina

Of all the St. Catherines, the most famous must be the highly romanticized Catherine of Alexandria, supposedly an Egyptian queen, whose beauty and philosophy attracted the attentions of the Emperor Maxentius. Having been converted to Christianity and—in a vision—mystically married to Christ, she did not reciprocate Maxentius' feelings. The emperor, determined to win her for his wife, sent 50 philosophers to reason her out of her faith, but she out-argued them, and they were all executed. She was then tortured and imprisoned. One attempt to break her spirit was made by trying to break her body on a spiked wheel. Instead it was the wheel that broke, killing some of the spectators. In the end, Catherine was decapitated, although legend has it that it was milk and not blood which poured from her neck. The Roman Martyrology no longer lists her.

There are many other St. Catherines whose historicity is certain; of these, St. Catherine of Siena is the most remarkable. Laywomen were rarely canonized in past centuries, yet Catherine was not only canonized in 1461 but also declared a Doctor of the Church, even though she was illiterate. Although she was not a member of an order, she became a third order Dominican and, in turn, attracted to herself a circle of admirers, who were called the "Caterinati," drawn from all walks of life. Gradually, Catherine became involved in the political and ecclesiastical scandal of the wars between Italian states and the pope and dictated many letters to religious and secular leaders, as well as mystical treatises. She received the stigmata and once had a vision of her mystical marriage to Christ.

Feast day: April 29

Symbols: a lily; the stigmata and crown of thorns; a wedding ring

Patron: of young girls, nurses, and Italy

St. Cecilia

Meaning: from the Latin, "dim-sighted"

Female variations: Cecille, Celine, Celia, Cis, Cicely, Cissie, Sheelagh, Sheila, Shelly, Zazilie, Zilla

Male variation: Cecil

Sadly, the legend of St. Cecilia is now considered to be just another Christian romance. Perhaps, though, we should be thankful that this woman did not suffer the torments of being suffocated by the steam in her own bath and then—when that proved useless—being left for three days to die of three sword strokes to her neck. The story is that Cecilia was a noble Roman Christian who vowed herself to virginity despite being married off to a man named Valerian. On their wedding night, she managed to convert him, and he was subsequently martyred together with his brother and a friend before the authorities made their assault on Cecilia.

Of course, it is Cecilia's connection with music that we are most familiar with. According to the story, it was through (or despite) the wedding music that Cecilia prayed to God for help, and she has become the muse of church musicians ever since. Whether or not there ever was a Cecilia is impossible to say. It may be that she was the wealthy Roman Cecilia who founded a church in Rome and was given an honorable burial there. At all events, the inspiration and the music are real enough.

Feast day: November 22

Symbols: an organ; a lute; a harp; two wreaths of roses and lilies

Patron: of musicians

St. Charles

Meaning: from Old German, "man"

Male variations: Carl, Carlo, Carlos, Carroll, Caryl, Chick, Chuck, Karel, Karl

Female variations: Charlotte, Carlotta, Charlene, Lola, Lolita, Lotte, Lottie, Tottie, Carla, Carol, Cheryl

We still tend to think of saints and martyrs as medieval and white —or even Roman and white—whereas, in fact, these past two centuries have seen more Christian martyrdoms than ever before, most of them in Third World countries. One of these, Charles Lwanga, was burned to death in 1886. He was one of many teenage boys kept by Mwanga, king of Uganda, in an "alternative" harem. Charles became a Christian and converted 22 of his friends, whereupon they were transported to Namugongo and executed. He is remembered on June 3 and honored as a patron of African boys.

The film *Black Robe* gave another side to the story of missionary stupidity and Native American sensitivity: Charles Garnier, a French priest who was murdered by the Iroquois while he was living and working in a Huron village in 1649, might have been the inspiration for it. His feast day is October 19.

St. Charles Borromeo, however, after whom so many of the other St. Charleses were named, was indeed medieval and white. After the rather scandalous start of being born to a Medici and a

Borromeo and becoming the owner of a rich abbey and then a cardinal by nepotism (literally—the gift given by his uncle, Pope Pius IV) before he was 23, Charles became a priest and bishop in his own right. Although he had a stammer, he preached tirelessly and set about reforming the church so rigorously that a monk of the Humilitati (an order which was losing money through these reforms) tried to assassinate him. When the plague broke out, he spent his energy and his personal fortune caring for the sick, and he also founded Sunday schools for the Confraternity of Christian Doctrine. If he had one indulgence, apparently it was the comparatively innocent one—at least by his ancestors' standards—of playing chess.

Feast day: November 4

Symbols: an orb and cross; the word *humilitas* (humility) with a crown

Patron: of Sunday school teachers, ordinands, and seminarians

St. Christina

Meaning: **from the Greek, "Christian"**

Female variations: Christiana, Christine, Chris, Christabel, Chrissie, Kirsten, Kirsty, Kristen, Krissy, Tina

Male variation: Christian

St. Christina the Astonishing is the most famous of several canonized Christians due to her peculiar psychic phenomena, all written down at the time by Cardinal James de Vitry. She was born in Liège, Belgium, in 1150; after a near-death experience—from which she "awoke" at her own funeral Mass—she flew up into the rafters of the church in disgust at the garlic-laden breath of the congregation. After her visions of hell and purgatory, she decided to give her life to prayer for the liberation of souls in purgatory, but the hypersensitivity to smell (especially the smell of men) never left her, and she went to extraordinary lengths (and heights) to avoid them. She is no longer in the Roman Martyrology. There are Christinas, such as St. Christina of Spoleto, February 13, whose feasts are celebrated.

St. Christopher

Meaning: **from the Greek, "Christ-bearer"**

Variations: Chris, Chrissie, Christie, Chrystal, Kester, Kit

Everyone has seen the little medals or statues showing the patron saint of travelers, St. Christopher. Their use stems from the fact that Christopher, so the story goes, was a giant of a man who longed to serve the greatest master; he entered the service of a king but left it when he saw the king abase himself before an evil wizard. Christopher then tried to serve the devil, but became disillusioned when he saw the devil cringe at the sight of a hermit's crucifix. The hermit lived beside a river and scratched a living ferrying people across, so Christopher stayed to help him.

One dark and stormy night, a tiny child came to Christopher and pleaded to be carried across. Against his better judgment, the giant took the child and entered the wild water. He found that he could barely stand while the weight of the child grew insupportable. When he had struggled desperately to the other side, the child told him that he was the Christ for whom Christopher was looking and that he had carried the weight of the whole world on his shoulder.

Even if this story is not true, it illustrates the literal meaning of the name "Christophoros" (Christ-bearer) which was borne by a martyr, probably in third-century Asia Minor. St. Christopher is still an important saint for travelers; perhaps he should also give courage to the growing numbers of unemployed people.

Feast day: July 25

Symbols: the Christ-child on his shoulder; a lantern; a palm tree and river

Patron: of all people who travel or work with transport, as well as those in danger of water, storms, or sudden death

St. Clare

Meaning: **from the Latin, "bright"**

Female variations: Claire, Clara, Chiara, Claribel, Clarice, Clarrie, Calinda, Clarissa

Male variations: Clare, Clarus

Clare, born in Assisi, Italy, scandalized her wealthy family—just as St. Francis had—by taking her faith too seriously and running away from them to live, like Francis and his fellow friars, with Lady Poverty for the love of God. Of course, the free Franciscan life on the road was not suitable for a woman of that time, and Clare had to be content to lead her own order of "Poor Ladies" in the church of San Damiano with a rule written for her by St. Francis.

Although she and her sisters could not travel with Francis, they shared his devotion to Christ and insisted on living in the greatest poverty. They embroidered church vestments and linen and gave their enclosed lives to prayer. Clare herself seems to have been as loved by her sisters as Francis was by his followers. Franciscan austerity was never imposed on other people, but it seems to have given freedom and joy to anyone who dared to risk it.

Feast day: August 11

Symbols: A chalice and host; a tall cross; a monstrance (the special gold or silver container for displaying the Blessed Sacrament); a lily; a ciborium (the covered chalice in which the consecrated bread is kept)

Patron: of embroiderers and those with eye troubles, also of television—either because her name means "light" or because one Christmas she was given a vision of the stable in Bethlehem

St. Clement

Meaning: **from the Latin, "merciful"**

Male variation: Clem

Female variations: Clementine, Clementia, Clementina, Clemency, Clem

The Clement from whom all other St. Clements take their name was the fourth pope, coming after Peter, Linus, and Cletus. St. Irenaeus tells us that "[Clement] had seen and consorted with the blessed apostles"; he may be the Clement mentioned in Philippians 4:3, but we do not know very much about his life. What we do have is his letter to the Corinthians, dealing with the troubled affairs of their church. Legends abound about him being sent to the marble mines of Russia and eventually martyred by being tied to an anchor and thrown into the sea. It is said that his tomb on the sea bed, made by angels, can be seen once a year at exceptionally low tides.

Feast day: November 23

Symbols: a fountain; an anchor; a tiara; a maniple (an ornamental band formerly worn on the left arm by the celebrant at Mass); a marble temple in the sea

Patron: of lighthouses, stonecutters, and blacksmiths

St. Crispin

Meaning: **from the Latin, "curled"**

Variations: Crispinian, Crispianius, Crispian

Crispin was a Roman shoemaker together with his brother, Crispinian. They set out on a missionary expedition to France with St. Quentin but were martyred at Soissons in 285. According to legend, their bodies were thrown into the sea and eventually found their way to Faversham in Kent. It may be that they were martyred in Rome, in fact, and their relics were brought to Soissons. Whatever the truth, they are still venerated as the patron saints of shoemakers and leather workers.

Feast day: October 25

Symbols: a shoe; a last (the wooden or metal form on which a shoe is fashioned)

Patron: of leather workers and cobblers

St. Crispina

Crispina was also martyred in the Roman persecutions. She was a Numidian woman, married and with children, who refused to sacrifice to pagan gods on behalf of the emperor and was therefore beheaded. Accounts of her trial exist, and she is mentioned several times by St. Augustine. Her feast day is December 5.

D

St. Damian

Meaning: from the Greek, a "tamer" or "guide"

Variations: Damyan, Dami, Damien, Damon

Like Crispin, Damian had a fraternal companion—Cosmas—although the names of Crispinian and Cosmas have not been as popular as their brothers'. Cosmas and Damian are highly venerated martyrs in the Eastern Church as twin brothers from Syria who practiced medicine and refused to accept fees for their help.

Feast day: September 26

Symbols: arrows; phials and jars; the rod of Aesculapius (the Roman god of medicine or healing)

Patron: of doctors, dentists, barbers, and pharmacists

St. Daniel

Meaning: from the Hebrew, "God judges"

Male variations: Danny, Dan, Deiniol

Female variations: Danielle, Daniella

Most Christians, perhaps, named in honor of Daniel are named after the Old Testament prophet who outfaced the lions in their den and who had such strange visions. There are actually three St. Daniels named after him: one, a medieval missionary to the Moors during the crusades; another, a French missionary to Senegal whose special love was for orphans and who died in 1936.

The third, the most famous Daniel of all, was the Stylite (or pillar-saint) who lived in the fifth century. He lived a perfectly ordinary monk's life until he paid two visits to Simon the Stylite, who lived as a hermit on top of a 60-foot pillar on Mount Telanissae. It fired his enthusiasm so much that he was ordained on top of a pillar of his own, given to him by the emperor Leo I, and lived there for 33 years. He came down only once, to reprimand the emperor Basilicus for supporting a heretical doctrine. Otherwise, he lived atop his pillar, healing the sick, giving spiritual direction, and preaching very good sermons.

Feast day: December 11

Symbol: a tall pillar

St. David

Meaning: **from the Hebrew, "beloved"**

Male variations: Dai, Dafydd, Dave, Davin, Davy, Dewi

Female variations: Davina, Davida, Davidina, Davinia, Davita, Veda, Vida, Vita

David is an Old Testament name, but its popularity is largely due to a Welsh saint, Dewi, known to non-Welsh speakers as "David." There are other canonized Davids, notably a Scottish king of the twelfth century, but it is St. David of Wales who is the best known. This David is reputed, in some historical accounts, to have descended from King Arthur; he was certainly revered all over the Celtic region. He became the first bishop in South Wales and founded a series of monasteries of extreme austerity—so much so that some accused him of being more in love with asceticism than Christ. His nickname ("the waterman") may derive from the fact that his rule forbade the drinking of wine; the tradition that he ate only bread and leeks (hence the Welsh emblem) is apocryphal.

Feast day: March 1

Symbols: a dove on a shoulder; a leek; a harp; a hill; fountains

Patron: of poetry and Wales

St. Dominic

Meaning: **from the Latin, "of the Lord"**

Male variations: Dom, Domenic, Domingo, Nick, Nicky

Female variations: Dominica, Dominique

Although there were several early martyrs called Dominica, it was the twelfth-century St. Dominic who inspired many more Dominics to become saints and martyrs. Dominic was a Spaniard whose religious energy sprang from his fights against heresy. Before he was born, his mother had a vision in which she saw her son as a dog holding a flaming torch; the nickname of the Dominican Order came to be "the hounds of God." Later, when he was christened, she saw a star shining on him. Dominic was to be, with Francis, the most influential saint of his era.

Dominic's first foundation was a convent for French nuns who had renounced the Albigensian heresy. For the rest of his life, he established and directed the Order of Preachers, the great counterpart to Francis' order. Between the two men, Western Christianity was reformed and rejuvenated by dusty friars traveling in poverty and preaching to ordinary people all over Europe. The popular image of Dominic was of a man as ruthless as the terrible inquisitions of the Cathars and Albigensians, which he supported, but apparently he was a hugely compassionate and intellectual man. He remained true to his ideal of personal poverty, dying in a borrowed habit and a borrowed bed because he possessed none of his own.

Feast day: August 8

Symbols: a lily; a greyhound; a book; a star on his forehead; a rosary; a dog holding a torch

Patron: of astronomy, friars, preachers, and the Dominican Republic

St. Dorothy

Meaning: from the Greek, "gift of God"

Variations: Dorothea, Dodie, Dolly, Dora, Doreen, Dorinda, Dorrit, Dory, Dot, Dottie

The martyr of the Diocletian persecution is a Christian heroine of a romance. The story goes that she was a beautiful girl of Cappadocia (Turkey) who was sentenced to death. As she was being led out to execution, a lawyer, Theophilus, jeered at her, asking her to send him fruit and flowers from the heavenly garden. After her death, a child appeared to him with a basket of roses and apples, adding—ominously—that Dorothy was waiting for him in the garden. Theophilus was converted and immediately executed too.

Feast day: February 6

Symbols: an angel with a basket of apples or roses; a sword; a crown

Patron: of florists and gardeners

E

St. Edmund

Meaning: **from Old English, "rich guardian"**

Variations: Eamon, Ed, Eddie, Edmond, Ned, Ted, Teddy

St. Edmund is largely forgotten now, except in the town of Bury St. Edmunds, Suffolk, where he is buried. But Edmund, king of the Angles and martyr, was once one of the greatest English saints and his shrine one of the richest in medieval Europe. The story of his martyrdom varies, but the best telling of it is by Julian Tennyson (*Suffolk Scene,* Alistair Press, 1987), one of Edmund's countrymen in our own century. The bare bones of it is that Edmund, the boy king, tried to defend his country from marauding Danes and was captured. Refusing to compromise his faith or the well-being of his people, Edmund was shot through with arrows in 870. The Danes then cut off his head and threw it away, but a wolf guarded it until it was discovered and reunited with his body.

Feast day: November 20

Symbols: arrows; a cudgel; a wolf

Patron: of East Anglia and wolves

St. Edward

Meaning: **from Old English, "rich guardian"**

Variations: Ed, Eddie, Ned, Neddy, Ted, Teddy

The first King Edward to be canonized was the unfortunate lad who, about 100 years after Edmund met his death, was murdered at the age of 16. Whether or not this was really a martyrdom, people reported many miracles happening about his grave and he was canonized soon after. His feast day is on March 18.

Edward the Confessor is chiefly remembered as the gentle but wise and effective king who succeeded to the throne of England in 1042. Even before his death, he was venerated for his holiness; it was of him that it was first said that to touch the king would cure scrofula, "the king's evil." Westminster Abbey is the beautiful church that we know today because of Edward's love for it. He refounded the small monastery, as it was then, and greatly enlarged the church where he, at his own wish, was buried on his death in 1066.

Feast day: October 13

Symbols: a ring in his hand; a scepter with a dove; a purse

St. Elizabeth

Meaning: **from the Hebrew, "God is fullness"**

Variations: Elisabeth, Eliza, Elly, Elsa, Elsie, Elspeth, Elise, Babette, Belle, Bess, Bessie, Beth, Betsy, Bettee, Bettina, Betty, Isabel, Isabella, Isobel, Ysabel, Libby, Libbie, Lib, Lillibet, Lisa, Lise, Liselotte, Lisette, Liz, Lizzie, Lizzy

The first Elizabeth in the Christian calendar was the cousin of Mary and the mother of St. John the Baptist. The story of her miraculous conception of John is told in the first pages of the Gospel according to St. Luke, and it mirrors the yet more miraculous birth of Christ. There are other traditions about her and her husband, Zechariah; whatever the truth of them, she is invoked as the patroness of all pregnant women for it was while he was in her womb that John first "leaped" in joyful recognition of Jesus.

Feast day: November 5

Symbols: Elizabeth herself greeting Mary and/or holding John the Baptist

Patron: of pregnant women

There have been many other St. Elizabeths since. One was Queen Elizabeth of Hungary, whose unhappy life as wife, mother, and queen was matched only by that of her great-niece, Queen Elizabeth of Portugal. Elizabeth of Hungary is remembered for her unceasing charity to the poor in spite of her husband's opposition and then, after his death, her own poverty. She died at the age of 24 in 1231. Her symbols are three crowns (as virgin, wife, and widow) and roses, a basket of bread, a baby in a cradle, a distaff, and bread and wine. Her feast day is November 17.

A later Elizabeth was the first American-born person to be canonized. Elizabeth Bayley Seton was born in 1774, was married and the mother of five children. Before her husband's death she founded a Protestant charity for women and children; after he died she became a Roman Catholic and founded a girls' school. She then became Mother Seton, the mother superior of a new congregation of nuns called the Daughters of Charity of St. Joseph. Her feast day is on January 4.

St. Emily

Meaning: from the French, possibly from Roman clan, Aemelius

Female variations: Em, Emalia, Emilia, Emmie, Emmy, Emilie

Male variation: Emil

One account of the first Blessed Emily tells that she was the first prioress of the first house of Dominican regular tertiaries. She was, at any rate, an Italian woman of the thirteenth century whose reputation for goodness—some say miracle-working power—has come down to us today. She is remembered on August 19. An Emily that followed her is Emily de Rodat, a Frenchwoman who had a sad and difficult life which, to some, made her a sad and difficult person. Nevertheless, in 1815 she opened a free school in Villefranche-de-Rouergue which became the congregation of the Holy Family at Villefranche and spread to other countries. Her feast day is on September 19.

Another St. Emily is also a Frenchwoman, Emily de Vialar, who founded in 1832 the Sisters of St. Joseph "of the Apparition." Despite her good work in her second foundation in Algeria, she was harried by its archbishop, excommunicated, and driven out of the country. Emily was proven innocent, however, and the congregation flourished, becoming internationally known for its charity and care of children. She herself was regarded as wise, sensitive, and utterly dedicated to her work, despite her own physical disabilities. Her feast day is on August 24.

St. Emma

Meaning: **from Old German, "universal"**

Variations: Em, Emmie, Erma, Imma, Irma

Little is known of St. Emma, who died in 1045, apart from the sad circumstances of her life. She was happily married to the landgrave of Friesach, Austria, and had two sons, but they were murdered and her husband died while away on a journey. Unlike many of the women who later became saints, widowhood was not delicious freedom but a terrible blow to Emma. She later founded a double monastery in Carinthia, Austria, and her feast day is celebrated on June 29.

St. Eric

Meaning: **from Old Norse, "ever ruling"**

Male variations: Erick, Rick, Rickie, Ricky

Female variations: Erica, Erika, Rickie, Rikkie

Eric IX became king of Sweden in 1150. He was a very pious, good Christian man and systematically set about ensuring that not only his own subjects but also the neighboring heathen Finns became Christians too. He codified Swedish law and built the first Swedish cathedral in Uppsala. He also defended his country against Finnish attack. Unfortunately, he was murdered in 1161 by a band of Danes abetted by some of his own treacherous countrymen.

Feast day: May 18

Symbols: three crowns and a banner; a fountain

Patron: of Sweden

F

St. Felix

Meaning: **from the Latin, "fortunate," "happy"**

There are over 60 saints called Felix recognized as martyrs by the Roman Catholic Church, but one of special interest to English people is the Burgundian who came as a missionary preacher to East Anglia and later became bishop of Dunwich, the mysterious cathedral town which was washed into the sea. He also gave his name to the port of Felixstowe. He died in 648 and his feast day is kept on March 8.

Felix of Nola lived three centuries earlier, near Naples, and became chaplain to his bishop, Maximus. During the persecutions carried out by Emperor Decius (249–251), Maximus went into hiding, but Felix was arrested and tortured until he escaped with the help of an angel. He, too, was forced to hide from his pursuers; he succeeded this time with the help of a spider which spun a web covering the entrance of the cave in which he hid. Later, he found Bishop Maximus and looked after him until he died, but he refused to be consecrated bishop himself. He was known for his generosity and compassion and, after his death, great miracle-working power.

Feast day: January 14

Symbols: a cluster of grapes; an angel; a spider's web

Patron: of all those who have been falsely accused

St. Felicity

Meaning: **from the Latin, "happiness"**

Variations: Felicia, Felice

The best known Felicity (one of the few women saints named in the Roman Mass) was the slave girl of a wealthy Carthaginian woman named Perpetua. She and her mistress were arrested in 202 and faced certain death for their faith. The only question was whether Felicity might not be spared since she was pregnant. Eager to face martyrdom with her mistress, Felicity prayed and was brought into premature labor, giving birth to a son. Touched by their faith, the prison governor was converted, but they were nevertheless both tortured and killed by wild beasts.

Feast day: March 7

Patron: of mothers and infertile women

St. Flora

Meaning: **Roman goddess of flowers or spring**

Variations: Fleur, Floella, Florella, Floretta, Florai, Floriane, Floris, Florrie

St. Flora and St. Mary are honored on November 24 for their refusal to give up their faith during the persecution of Christians by the Moors in Spain. They were beheaded in Cordoba in 851. A later Flora (of Beaulieu) was a nun of the Order of St. John of Jerusalem, near Rocamadour in France, but the strange accounts of her spiritual life are uncertain. She died in 1347 and her feast day is October 5.

St. Frances

Meaning: from the Latin, "from France" or "a free citizen"

Variations: Francesca, Fan, Fanny, Francine, Françoise, Frank, Fran, Franny, Zissie

Frances Xavier Cabrini was the first citizen of the USA to be canonized, although she was Italian, born in 1850. Her first congregation was one of missionary nuns in Lombardy; she was then sent to America by Pope Leo XIII. Once here, Frances founded an orphanage for the children of Italian immigrants at West Park and hospitals in New York and Chicago. She continued working throughout the American continents, in Nicaragua, Chile, Argentina, Brazil, and Costa Rica, until her death in 1917 in Chicago.

Feast day: November 13

Patron: of hospital managers, emigrants, and immigrants

St. Francis

Variations: Fran, Frank, Franklin, Francisco

Francis of Assisi was the first saint from which very many have taken their names, although "Francesco" was just a nickname. Born in 1181, Francis (or John) was dazzled not only by the courtly romances of France but by chivalry and adventure too. However, his joie de vivre and imagination were caught up in a completely new adventure: that of trying to live the gospel as it was actually written. It sounds simple but in medieval Italy it was revolutionary.

Although Francis' family were Christians, they were not prepared to see their wealth given away impulsively. Francis kissed lepers, delighted in being mocked or even attacked, lived only on what he was given as alms, and took God's command to rebuild the church equally literally: he found a small ruined church and began to restore it, stone by stone. The friars who joined him, the animals and birds who heard him preach, the women who formed his second order of Poor Clares, and the many ordinary people who became tertiaries all show how Francis' extraordinary gifts and determination to live the gospel as perfectly as possible did, indeed, rebuild the church in the twelfth century. He was the first saint to experience the strange phenomenon of the stigmata—Christ's wounds on the cross—in his own body. The influence of Francis is still being felt in the church today, especially where it works to protect the natural world or help the poor.

Feast day: October 4

Symbols: birds; animals; a winged crucifix with five rays; a crown of thorns; a lighted lamp; fine clothes and a bag of gold at his feet

Patron: of birds and animals, the Green movement, and Italy

G

St. Gabriel

Meaning: **from the Hebrew, "God is strong"**

Male variations: Gabby, Gabe

Female variations: Gabrielle, Gabriella, Gabby, Gabey

When people want to suggest someone who is absolutely perfect, they often invoke the archangel Gabriel, who does, of course, have the edge on most saints simply by virtue of being an archangel. It was Gabriel who announced God's plan of action for the salvation of the world to the Virgin Mary, but he had previously appeared to Daniel and to Zechariah, and at the birth of Christ he undoubtedly joined the angels in their exultant *Gloria in excelsis Deo.* Because of this, Gabriel is thought of as the communicator *in excelsis* and is the patron of all who work in communications. He is also honored by Muslims as the one who dictated the Quran to Mohammed.

Feast day: September 29

Patron: of diplomats, communications workers, and women in childbirth

St. Gemma

Meaning: **from the Latin, "jewel"**

Gemma Galgani was a young Tuscan servant born in 1878 to a poor pharmacist. She longed to enter the order of the Passionist nuns but was chronically ill with spinal tuberculosis. Although she later believed that she had been cured miraculously by the intervention of St. Gabriel Possenti, she was still too weak. Nevertheless, she led an extraordinary life—alternating between mystical and demonic states, receiving the marks of the stigmata, and often behaving in a way she could only explain as being possessed by demons. In between these periods, Gemma was considered to be exceptionally holy and patient in her suffering, and it was for these qualities that she was canonized after her death at the age of 25.

Feast day: April 11

Patron: of pharmacists

St. George

Meaning: **from the Greek, "farmer"**

Male variations: Dod, Doddy, Geordie, Yorick, Jorge

Female variations: Georgia, Georgette, Georgiana, Georgina, Georgie, Gina

There is so much skepticism about the story of George and the dragon that many people have begun to doubt his very existence, but it is probable that St. George was a soldier of the third or fourth century, martyred in the Diocletian persecutions at Lydda in Palestine. Certainly, he became a widely venerated saint, especially among soldiers, and especially in the Eastern Church. The legend about the princess and the dragon was probably added in the medieval period, fond as people then were about stories of chivalry and romance. According to legend, George was a knight from Cappadocia who, when traveling through Silene in Libya, heard that the princess was to be the next victim of a fierce dragon which was gradually devouring all the young virgins of the place. George offered to go to the dragon in her place. There was a bloody fight between George and the dragon, but the former beheaded the latter, and the townspeople were so impressed that thousands became Christians on that day.

True or not, it is a story about courage and goodness which still catches the imagination, and the English still stoutly claim his patronage. The Orthodox and Roman Catholic Churches continue to venerate him and celebrate his feast.

Feast day: April 23

Symbols: a dead dragon; a broken wheel; a white flag with a red cross

Patron: of knights and soldiers (especially cavalry), Boy Scouts, riders, England, Portugal, and Germany

St. Gerald

Meaning: from Old German, "spear wielder"

Male variations: Gary, Gerrie, Gerry, Jerold, Jerrie, Jerry

Female variations: Geralda, Geraldine, Gerrie, Gerry, Jerrie, Jerry

Gerald of Aurillac, France, is one of the few laymen canonized for the holiness of his daily life. He was born in 855 into the aristocracy and would later administer his estates with justice, great generosity, and compassion for the poor. Although he did not feel free enough to renounce the world himself, he lived according to a rule and founded a Benedictine monastery. His feast day is October 13. Another Frenchman, Gerald of Sauve-Majeure, lived in the eleventh century. He first became abbot at Laon and then—finding the rule there too lax—at his own foundation at Sauve-Majeure. His feast day is April 5.

St. Gilbert

Meaning: **from Old German, "bright pledge"**

Male variations: Bert, Bertie, Berty, Gib, Gibb, Gil

Female variations: Gilberta, Gilberte

Gilbert of Sempringham is particularly interesting because he founded the only medieval order which originated in England—the Gilbertines—and also because he lived to the age of 106 at a time when the average life expectancy was about a quarter of that. Gilbert was born in Sempringham, Lincolnshire, in 1189 and became the vicar of the parish. Awhile later, when seven women asked him to write a rule for them to live in community there, Gilbert initiated a widespread order of men and women, lay and ordained, for work in hospitals and orphanages. Gilbert seems to have been a man of courage—he dared to help St. Thomas à Becket in his quarrel with King Henry II—and a man of humility as well, for when he went blind in his old age, he was content to step down as abbot and live on in his community as an ordinary brother.

Feast day: February 16

Symbol: a model of a church

St. Giles

Meaning: **from the Greek, "shield," "protection"**

Male variations: Aegidius, Egidius, Gyles

Female variations: Egidia, Giles

St. Giles, a much-loved saint in Britain, is one of the medieval saints who are particularly associated with animals. The story goes that he was a French hermit living in Saint-Gilles, near Arles, before the ninth century. He used to be fed by a deer who gave him her milk. One day, however, King Wamba of the Visigoths came crashing through the forest on a hunt; the deer sought refuge with Giles and sheltered in the saint's arms; the king tried to shoot the deer but found he had shot and wounded St. Giles instead. Perhaps out of remorse, Wamba gave Giles land on which he subsequently built a monastery.

Feast day: September 1

Symbol: a red deer killed with arrows

Patron: of cripples and beggars, breast-feeding mothers, and hermits. He is also invoked by women who wish to conceive.

St. Gregory

Meaning: **from the Greek, "watchman"**

Male variations: Gregor, Greer, Greg, Gregg

Female variations: Greer, Gregoria

Gregory (540–604) is one of the great figures in the Western Church. Born into a wealthy family and becoming a very successful chief civil magistrate in Rome, he subsequently devoted much of his wealth to the founding of monasteries, eventually renouncing his worldly life and becoming a monk. Ten years later, in 590, he was the first monk ever to be elected pope.

Perhaps his most famous saying was made on passing through the slave market. He was admiring some blond children and asked of what race they were. On being told that they were Angles, he protested, "Not Angles but angels!" On learning that the Angles of England were pagans, he put plans in order that Augustine should lead a mission there.

He has affected our lives in many ways, being a keen statesman and having had a great influence on the emerging Europe of his time. He shaped the way clergy—especially bishops—came to see their ministry and famously reorganized the church's patterns of worship and music. What we know as Gregorian chant was written down and systematized under his supervision.

Feast day: September 3

Symbols: a dove; an altar; an ancient manuscript of music

Patron: of music, popes, and schools

St. Guy

Meaning: **possibly from the Latin, "life," or from Old German, "wood" or "wild"**

Guy of Anderlecht was a Belgian peasant in the tenth century who, poor though he was, resolved to renounce the pursuit of money and become a hermit. He eventually became the sacristan of a church at Laeken, where he lived happily until he was persuaded by a merchant to invest the little money he had left. His hope was that it would raise money to help the poor, but it ended disastrously with the ship his goods were on going down. Thoroughly disillusioned, Guy left Laeken on a pilgrimage and spent years wandering through Europe to Rome and Jerusalem, returning to Laeken to die. Although he is credited with many miracles, it was the events surrounding his burial at Anderlecht which seemed to confirm his local popularity. When a horse kicked his grave (or did something even less respectful, according to some sources), it was immediately struck dead. This makes him, oddly enough, the patron saint of horses.

Feast day: September 12

Patron: of horses

H

St. Helen

Meaning: "woman of Greece"

Variations: Aileen, Eileen, Elaine, Eleanor, Elena, Elinor, Ella, Ellen, Ellie, Helena, Ilene, Lana, Lena, Leonora, Nell, Nellie, Nelly

St. Helen is always thought of as the woman who found the cross on which Christ was crucified. Born in about 255 in Drepanum, Asia Minor, Helen was probably just an ordinary poor girl until she happened to attract the attention of a Roman officer stationed there called Constantius. She went with him to Rome and gave birth to a son. More was to come, however, for Constantius became emperor and tried to divorce his humble wife, banishing her from Rome. When Helen's son Constantine inherited his father's empire, Helen was brought back again and crowned as an empress.

Constantine won a famous victory after having had a vision of the cross of Christ; after that, Christianity became legal in the Roman Empire. Helen embraced the faith and went on pilgrimage to the Holy Land, where she studied the ancient sites and founded many churches, as well as helping the poor. Whether or not the story is true about her finding the cross buried near Calvary and finding the nails and seamless robe, her faith, devotion, and charity are undoubted.

Feast day: August 18

Symbols: a crown; a cross; a hammer and nails; an open book and a crown

Patron: of archaeologists

St. Henry

Meaning: from Old German, "home ruler"

Male variations: Hal, Hank, Harry

Female variations: Etta, Ettie, Hattie, Henrietta, Hettie, Hetty

Henry II (born in 973) was a Bavarian prince and later Holy Roman Emperor. His tutor was St. Wolfgang of Regensburg; Henry apparently had a vision of Wolfgang after his death, portending his own coronation. He was also a friend of St. Odilo of Cluny, and it was said that he, too, wanted to be a monk and therefore never consummated his marriage with St. Cunegund. It seems that Henry worked with zeal for German unity and the church's reorganization.

Feast day: July 13

Symbols: a sword and a church; a lily; a crown; a dove on an orb

Patron: of Finland

St. Hilary

Meaning: from the Latin, "cheerful"

Male variations: Hilaire, Hillary

Female variations: Hilaira, Illaria, Yllaria

There were five Hilarys canonized in the early church, but it is Hilary of Poitiers who is best known to us, giving his name in England to the second term in the academic year—the Hilary Term—since the spring term would begin around the time of his feast day, to the Law Courts and some universities. Hilary was born about 315 into a wealthy pagan family of Poitiers; after his conversion to Christianity he was consecrated as bishop (although he was married and a father). He is chiefly remembered for his great theological writings against the Arian heresy which was exerting influence in the Church at that time. Arius taught that Jesus Christ was human, not divine, whereas orthodox Christianity has always believed Jesus Christ to be both human and divine. In fact, Hilary was such a fierce defender of the Trinity that he was exiled from his diocese and sent to Phrygia by Emperor Constantius II (who happened to be an Arian himself). This ploy backfired, for Hilary proceeded to dig deeper into Greek theology, becoming even more convinced by orthodox Christian doctrine—and was not afraid to say so. In the end, the Arians sent him back to his diocese, labeling him a mischief-maker.

After he died, his bed was set up in the cathedral of Poitiers and was known as Hilary's Cradle. It was thought that anyone who could be made to sleep a night in it would be cured of insanity. Hilary also was reputed to have cleared an island of snakes and thus is often invoked against snakebite.

Feast day: January 13

Symbols: a child in a cradle; a trumpet; a serpent on a stick

Patron: of slow learners, the mentally ill, and lawyers

St. Hilda

Meaning: **from Old German, "battle"**

Variations: Hilde, Hildy, Hylda

Hilda was a noblewoman of Northumbria, christened at the age of 13 with her great-uncle, King Edwin, in 627. Her vocation to the religious life came relatively late, but when she was 33 she was installed as abbess of a monastery in Hartlepool by St. Aidan. Shortly after this, Hilda founded a double monastery at Whitby which became one of the largest and most important religious foundations in Britain. The Venerable Bede writes about her and some of the eminent people who lived there, including St. John of Beverley and Caedmon, believed to be the author of the first English religious lyrics. A historic conference took place at Whitby in 664 to decide whether the English church should follow the Celtic or Roman church calendar. Apart from being formidably efficient and wise, Hilda was also very lovable, according to Bede.

Feast day: November 17

Symbols: snakes; a bird; a crosier; a model of Whitby Abbey

St. Hugh

Meaning: **from Old German, "understanding"**

Male variations: Hew, Huey, Hughie, Hugo, Hughes, Huw

Female variation: Huguette

St. Hugh of Grenoble was the beloved bishop of that city, whose personal holiness was combined with a great determination to improve both the practical and devotional life of the people in his care. He was once a pupil of St. Bruno, and it was he who gave Bruno and his companions the land on which to build the great Cistercian monastery at La Grande Chartreuse. His feast day is celebrated on April Fools' Day, and his symbols in art are a branch and seven stars, lanterns, or three flowers.

St. Hugh of Lincoln was, despite his name, another Frenchman, born in 1135—three years after his compatriot's death. Like many other bishops, Hugh was appointed by a king hopeful of making friends in high places; like many other kings, Henry II was disappointed. In fact, Hugh turned out to be so firm in the defense of his people against the greed and arrogance of their royal masters that he was called Hammerking. He may have called himself "peppery," but he was greatly admired for his courage in standing up to Henry II, Richard, and John. Not only did he fight royal oppression but he was remarkable for his defense of the Jews in his city at a time when persecution was common. He was known as a kind and tender man with time for the poor, for playing with children and caring for the ill. He kept many pets, including a wild swan who would bury its head in Hugh's wide sleeves and follow him everywhere about his manor, returning to the wild when Hugh was away from home.

Feast day: November 17

Symbol: a swan

Patron: of swans

St. James

Meaning: from the Hebrew, "Jacob" or "supplanter"

Male variations: Jake, Jamey, Jamie, Jaime, Jay, Jem, Jemmy, Jim, Jimmy, Hamish, Seamus, Diego

Female variations: Jamesina, Jacoba, Jacqueline, Jacquetta, Jackie, Jacklyn, Jem

While Jacob is one of the Old Testament heroes whose very name —supplanter—tells us that he was not very saintly, there are two Jameses who were apostles—the Greater and the Less—and became saints. James the Greater is perhaps more familiar, being the brother of John, son of Zebedee, and one of the inner circle of disciples. Some believe that James and John may even have been cousins of Jesus, if Salome was their mother and was Mary's sister. James and John, together with Peter, were the disciples Jesus called to witness his transfiguration and to be with him during his agony in the garden of Gethsemane. The Acts of the Apostles tells us that James was the first of the Twelve to be martyred—he was executed by King Herod Agrippa I in 44. The legend is that his body was miraculously transferred to Santiago de Compostela, Spain. The great cathedral there became, with Jerusalem and Rome, one of the main centers of pilgrimage so that James' symbol, the cockleshell, became the badge for all pilgrims.

Feast day: July 25

Symbols: a pilgrim's staff, hat, cloak, wallet, purse, and cockleshell; keys; a white horse and white flag

Patron: of soldiers and cavalry, veterans, furriers, Spain, Guatemala, and Nicaragua

There are actually two Jameses we celebrate on May 3. James, son of Alphaeus, was an apostle, but he is not believed to be "the Lord's brother," mentioned several times in the New Testament. The latter became the leader of the church in Jerusalem after Pentecost and was stoned to death in about 62. In Mark 15:40, the evangelist calls this second James "the younger," but since these two Jameses have been traditionally identified as the same person, it is the apostle who is called "the Less."

Feast day: May 3

Symbols: a windmill; a halberd; three stones; bread

Patron: of the dying

St. Jane

Meaning: from the Hebrew, "God is gracious"

Variations: Jan, Janet, Janey, Janie, Janice, Joan, Sheena, Sheenagh, Sian, Sine, Sinead

Jane is one of the feminine forms of John, so a Jane or Joan might take one of the many St. Johns for her patron. There is, however, a very attractive St. Jane whose life might be an inspiration for any woman because it combined marriage and motherhood with great holiness and administrative skill. Jane Frances de Chantal (1572–1641) was a well-born Frenchwoman of Dijon. She married when she was 20 and had four children; unfortunately, after eight happy years, she was widowed. She later began to develop her spiritual life under the direction of St. Francis de Sales. Three years later, he asked her to become the superior of a new order for women which would foster the vocations of widows like herself or women whose age or health would not permit them to join other, more austere orders. Therefore, Jane became the foundress of the Order of the Visitation; it grew so fast that there were 80 houses by the time she died. Jane was the grandmother of that spirited woman of letters, Madame de Sévigné; according to St. Vincent de Paul, Jane was "one of the holiest people I have ever met on this earth."

Feast day: December 12

St. Jerome

Meaning: **from the Greek, "sacred name"**

Variations: Geronimo, Gerrie, Gerry, Jerry

St. Jerome is the saint always portrayed with a lion because of the delightful story about how he bravely removed a thorn from its paw, setting the lion to watch over his recalcitrant donkey. Jerome was not just a desert hermit and animal lover, however. He is also remembered as a Doctor of the Church because of his outstanding scholarship. In 382, Jerome became secretary to Pope St. Damasus, who set him the extraordinary labor of translating the Greek and Hebrew books of the Bible into Latin, which was becoming the universal language of the Western Church. Although he was notoriously vitriolic about marriage, Jerome conceived a great friendship for a Roman widow, Paula, and her daughters, and they went to live in Bethlehem. With Paula's money, they were able to found a double monastery, hospice, and school. He died there in 420.

Feast day: September 30

Symbols: a lion; an inkhorn and pen; a fox; a hare; a partridge; an open Bible; a fawn

Patron: of librarians and scholars

St. Joan

Meaning: **from the Hebrew, "God is gracious"**

Variations: Jan, Janet, Janice, Janie, Janine, Jean, Jeanette, Jennet, Jennie, Jenny, Jessie, Jinny, Joanna, Joanne, Juanna, Joni, Netta, Nettie, Sheena, Sian, Sine, Sinead, Siobhan

Joan is the name of several French saints, the most famous of whom is, of course, Joan of Arc. This illiterate teenage peasant girl was prompted by heavenly voices, those of St. Michael, St. Catherine, and St. Margaret, to crown the Dauphin at Rheims and to lead his troops into battle. When Charles VII's courage failed, things went against the French. Joan was captured by the Burgundians, who were allied with the English, and sold to them for a show trial. It is often forgotten, however, that her canonization was not for her patriotism or her courage, but for her faithfulness and obedience to God. She was only 19 when she chose death by burning rather than collusion with political lies.

Feast day: May 30

Symbols: a fleur-de-lys; armor; a sword; a flag with the fleur-de-lys; a tunic; a stake

Patron: of France

St. John

Meaning: **from the Hebrew, "God is gracious"**

Variations: Evan, Ewan, Iain, Ian, Juan, Jack, Jan, Jevan, Jock, Johnny, Owen, Sean, Shaun, Zane

There are at least 64 Johns in the Roman Martyrology as well as many other fascinating people like the Curé d'Ars and St. John of the Cross; the number of different forms of the name show how popular it was and still is. But it was from St. John the Apostle and Evangelist and, to a lesser extent, St. John the Baptist, that all Johns took their inspiration.

St. John the Evangelist was the brother of James, son of Zebedee, and perhaps even the cousin of Jesus. He was certainly one of the three disciples who were called to be with Jesus during his transfiguration and the agony in the garden of Gethsemane, and tradition has it that he was "the disciple whom Jesus loved," mentioned in his Gospel. It was he who received Jesus' charge to look after Mary, his mother, and he who, as tradition has it, gave us the majestic fourth Gospel, as well as other letters in the New Testament. It is said that he lived for many years on Patmos, Greece, and later at Ephesus, Turkey, where he died.

Feast day: December 27

Symbols: a cup and a serpent; an eagle; a serpent on a sword; a scroll of his Gospel

Patron: of writers and Turkey

John the Baptist has a rather different reputation from that of the gentle old man of Ephesus. Luke's Gospel account certainly portrays him as the cousin of Jesus, but he seems to have been a rough and ready man. As a baby in the womb he greeted Jesus and later became the voice crying in the wilderness, "Prepare the way of the Lord," as foretold in Malachi 3:1. His life baptizing people in the Jordan was as dramatic in its ending as it was at the beginning when an angel appeared to his father. He was imprisoned and beheaded during Herod's birthday feast at the instigation of Herod's wife and her daughter, who danced for the king.

Feast day: June 24 (the old Midsummer Day) and August 29

Symbols: a camel-hair tunic; a locust; his head on a platter; a lamb; a lamb on a book with seven seals; an open Bible; a scroll with the words *Ecce Agnus Dei* (Behold the Lamb of God)

Patron: of motorways, road construction workers, leather- and wool-workers

St. Joseph

Meaning: **from the Hebrew, "may God increase"**

Male variations: José, Beppo, Jo, Joe, Joey

Female variations: Josephine, Fifi, Jo, Jolene, Josie, Josette, Pepita, Pepina

Little is known about St. Joseph, the carpenter who was betrothed to Mary and became the earthly father of Jesus. Legend has it that he was an old man when he married Mary, who was already pregnant. He was reassured in a dream by an angel who proclaimed his betrothed's chastity. Certainly, the Gospels are largely silent about him, but the care he took of the mother and child and his obedience to God's will are clear.

Feast day: March 19 and May 1

Symbols: a carpenter's square, saw, axe, and hatchet; a staff; a dove

Patron: of carpenters, fathers, house-hunters, Austria, Belgium, Canada, Mexico, Peru, and Vietnam

Other St. Josephs include Joseph of Arimathea, the devout Jew who offered his own expensive rock-tomb to shelter Jesus' body; he is thus patron saint of undertakers and cemetery staff. He has always had a place in English affections because of the legend that he came to Glastonbury after the resurrection, bringing the chalice used at the Last Supper (Arthur's Holy Grail), and planting his staff, which grew into a flowering hawthorn tree. His symbols are a thorn tree, a box of ointment, a vase, and the Holy Grail; his feast day is celebrated on August 31.

A more disorderly but engaging St. Joseph was the young Franciscan friar of Cupertino, Italy, who was only ordained by mistake, since he was thought to be mentally retarded. He may have been, but he was full of irrepressible joy and a strange ability to foretell events, which eventually persuaded the church hierarchy that he was a saint. Rather more alarmingly, St. Joseph became notorious for his astonishing habit of levitating, especially when moved by Christmas carols. Although this attracted many visitors, his superiors were not pleased. He is now, appropriately enough, patron of astronauts and all involved in aviation. His feast day is September 18.

St. Julia

Meaning: **possibly from a Roman family name, meaning "downy"**

Variations: Gillian, Gill, Gillie, Jill, Jilly, Juliana, Jules, Julie, Juliet, Julitta

St. Julia of Corsica was a Christian from Carthaginia who was sold as a slave in 439. She was taken to Corsica by her master, who was proud of her goodness and beauty, and found herself being coveted by Felix, the pagan governor. She refused to renounce her faith or her virginity and was tortured and crucified.

Feast day: May 22

Symbols: a cross and ropes; a scourge; a dove

Patron: of Corsica

St. Julian

Meaning: **possibly from a Roman family name, meaning "downy"**

Variations: Gillean, Julio, Julius, Jolyon, Jolyan, Jules

St. Julian the Hospitaler is the patron of many churches, hospitals, and charities in Europe because of the strange story about him in the medieval *Golden Legend* (drawn up by Jacob of Voraigne between 1255–1266, containing lives of saints and short treatises on Christian festivals). Julian was horrified to discover that it was predicted that he would kill his parents, so he sent himself into exile. He eventually married, but his loving parents searched for and found him, only to be killed by him in a terrible mistake, just as the prediction had said.

Full of terrible remorse, Julian and his wife abandoned their castle and wealth and set up a pilgrim's hospice and ferry on the banks of a dangerous river. Shortly before their deaths, Julian rowed an angel—well-disguised as a poor, ill pilgrim—across the river. Before the angel disappeared, he assured Julian that God had seen his penitence and forgiven the murder. Julian is no longer in the Roman Martyrology, but there are other Julians; for instance, St. Julian of Cuenca's feast is on January 28.

St. Justin & St. Justina

Meaning: **from the Latin, "just"**

Female variation; Justine

Justin was one of the first Christian philosophers. He was born in 100, in Samaria, to a Greek-speaking family. Justin traveled to Alexandria, the great city of learning, where he studied many different philosophies but was eventually baptized a Christian. He wrote many treatises, some of which survive, and traveled to many countries, preaching the gospel (as a layman) to pagans and Jews. On his second visit to Rome, he was denounced to the authorities and executed. Justin's symbols are quill pens and a sword, and he is remembered on June 1, especially by philosophers.

Three centuries later, Justine was to prove that right-minded women could be equally brave. She was a beautiful pagan princess who was martyred on her way to join the bishop of Padua. Legend has it that it was her knees which left two dents in the stones of the bridge there as she knelt to pray for help during her arrest. Her symbol is a unicorn, the friend of virgins, and her feast is celebrated on October 7.

K

St. Kevin

Meaning: **from Old Irish, "handsome at birth"**

Male variation: Kevan

St. Kevin (or Coemgen) was a very attractive character—legends abound about how he loved and was beloved of birds and animals. Some legends can be found in Helen Waddell's book *Beasts and Saints* (Eerdmans, 1996); one tells of how he remained in prayer for so long that a blackbird nested in his hand. Kevin refused to move until she had hatched her brood and the fledglings were safely launched. St. Kevin was born in Leinster and founded a monastery at Glendalough, County Wicklow, where he died in 618.

Feast day: June 3

Patron: of Ireland

St. Kieran

Meaning: **from Old Irish, "black-haired"**

Male variations: Ciaran, Kerry

Female variations: Kerry, Ciara, Ciaran

St. Kieran, or Ciaran, was another Irish saint. He was born in County Meath and was sent as a boy to become a monk in St. Finnian's monastery. From there, he went to study under St. Enda and then left to found his own monastery at Clonmacnoise, County Offaly, which later became one of the greatest of Ireland's places of holiness and learning. He died in about 549; literally, just before his death, he seemed to be coming to life again—perhaps one of the earliest recorded near-death-experiences.

Feast day: September 9

L

St. Lawrence

Meaning: **from the Latin, "of Laurentium" or "a bay tree"**

Male variations: Lanty, Larry, Laurence, Laurie, Laurien, Lawrie, Lonnie, Lorrie

Female variations: Laurencia, Laura, Laurel, Lauren, Laurie, Loretta, Lori, Lorrie

Extraordinary stories are told of this third-century martyr, and traditional Catholics believe he is well worth cultivating because he is thought to hold the privilege of rescuing a soul from purgatory every Friday. This was awarded to him in recognition of the particularly horrible martyrdom he suffered, which was—among many other tortures—to be roasted to death on a gridiron.

Lawrence was one of the seven deacons of Rome, appointed to serve the poor and needy; he also served Pope Sixtus II as his librarian. When Sixtus was arrested and put to death in one of Emperor Valerian's persecutions, Lawrence was commanded to hand over all the wealth of the church. He asked for three days' grace and then presented to the authorities a huge crowd of poor and handicapped people, widows and orphans, saying, "Here is the church's treasure." This so annoyed the Roman authorities that Lawrence was also arrested. The story goes that he never lost his serenity throughout the dreadful agonies to which he was subjected; as he was stretched out on the gridiron his last words were, "Turn me over, I'm cooked on this side."

Feast day: August 10

Symbols: a dalmatic (the robe a deacon wears for Mass); a thurible or censer (container for burning incense); a gridiron; a plate of money

Patron: of cooks, librarians, and poor people; also Sri Lanka

St. Leo

Meaning: **from the Latin, "lion"**

Male variations: Leoline, Leon, Leonard, Lionel

Female variations: Leonarda, Leona, Leonora, Leonore, Leonie

Leo I was one of the greatest popes of the church, being a learned theologian and an able, energetic, and brave leader—for instance, he personally persuaded Attila the Hun not to invade Rome in 452 and prevented a massacre when Genseric (king of the Vandals) and his men eventually succeeded in invading Rome in 455. It was Leo's *Tome* which finally quashed the Monophysite heresy (that is, that Christ's earthly self was always of a divine nature and therefore could not really suffer or die), which was becoming popular in the West at that time.

Feast day: November 10

Symbols: a statue of Mary; a pick-axe; a horse; Attila kneeling

St. Leonard

Meaning: **from the Latin and Old German, "lion bold"**

Male variations: Lionel, Len, Lenard, Lennie, Lenny, Leo, Leon

Female variations: Leo, Leona, Leonarda, Leonora, Leonore, Leonie

A popular medieval saint in France, Germany, and Britain, little is known for sure about St. Leonard. A book written about him in the eleventh century *(The Life of St. Leonard)* recounts that he was a hermit who refused a bishopric and went to live in a forest in southern France. One day, King Clovis and his wife were riding through the forest when the queen, who was pregnant, unexpectedly went into labor. St. Leonard gave them shelter and delivered the baby, and the king was so thankful that he granted him as much land as he could ride around on a donkey in one night and a pardon for any prisoners he visited. Leonard built a monastery on the land he was granted, and many of the men freed by the royal pardon joined Leonard there. It is thought that his monastery also became a popular shrine for returning crusaders, especially those who had been taken prisoner and had invoked Leonard's aid for their release.

Feast day: November 6

Symbols: a chain with manacles; broken chains; a fountain

Patron: of women in childbirth and prisoners, especially prisoners of war

St. Louis

Meaning: **from old German, "glorious battle"**

Variations: Lew, Lewes, Lewis, Lou, Louie, Ludovic, Luis, Aloys, Aloysius

The meaning of Louis has a certain irony in the case of St. Louis, King Louis IX of France. Although he led two crusades, the first ended in defeat and his own capture, and the second caused his death from dysentery at Tunis in 1270. On the other hand, his efforts to drive the English from France were more successful and he managed to make a treaty with his brother-in-law, Henry III. Louis was a man of great integrity, managing to balance the demands of kingship with his spiritual life as a third order Franciscan. It is well known that he had a particular distaste for bad language and would not tolerate it in those around him. He was happily married to Margaret of Provence, by whom he had eleven children. His greatest monument is the stunning Sainte-Chapelle in Paris, which was built to house a relic believed to have been the original crown of thorns.

Feast day: August 25

Symbols: a crown and scepter tipped with the Hand of God; a fleur-de-lys; a dove

Patron: of masons and sculptors

St. Louise

Variations: Loise, Lois, Louie, Louisa, Lu, Luisa, Lulu

St. Louise, a compatriot of King Louis but born 300 years later in 1591, was a wealthy young widow. Her confessor, St. Vincent de Paul, saw potential in her for great spiritual development rather than mere charity, and Louise began to work with the poorest of Paris. Gradually, she attracted other women to her and she founded a new congregation, the Daughters of Charity, "whose convent is the sickroom and whose cloister is the streets." Their work spread throughout France, but it was their Hôtel Dieu in Paris which inspired Florence Nightingale to develop her own hospitals 300 years later.

Feast day: March 15

Patron: of widows, orphans, and social workers

St. Lucy

Meaning: **from the Latin, "light"**

Female variations: Lucasta, Lucia, Lucille, Lucinda, Lucie, Luz

Male variations: Lucian, Lucien, Lucius

"Lucy" means "light" and it may be for this reason that her feast day falls near the winter solstice. It may be, though, because legend has it that she plucked out her eyes and presented them on a plate to the man whose thwarted lust drove him to denounce her as a Christian. Whatever the truth of that story, it seems that Lucy was a beautiful young girl of Syracuse in Sicily, living in the third or fourth century. She accompanied her suffering mother to the shrine of St. Agnes, where their prayers for a cure were answered. This miracle persuaded Lucy to consecrate her life to God and to give away all her wealth. Her fiancé betrayed her, and she was cruelly tortured and executed. Lucy is a greatly loved saint in Sweden, and her feast day is celebrated with special food and processions of girls with wreaths of candles on their heads.

Feast day: December 13

Symbols: a lamp; a dagger; three crowns; two oxen; a cup; ropes

Patron: of all who work with lights, glaziers, and those with eye trouble

St. Luke

Meaning: **from the Latin, "of Lucania"**

Variations: Lucas, Luck

By tradition, Luke was a Greek-speaking Gentile, and besides writing the third Gospel, he was Paul's "beloved physician" and also a painter. Although scholars now find as many Hebrew themes in the Gospel as Gentile ones, Luke's work is still characterized by its emphasis on the emotional and its sympathy for women. Again, traditionally, Luke is believed to have painted Mary's portrait and recounted his version of the nativity from her own memories.

Feast day: October 18

Symbols: a winged ox; bottles of medicine; a book and pen; brushes and a palette; a picture of Mary

Patron: of doctors, painters, butchers, glassmakers, goldsmiths, lace makers, and lawyers

M

St. Madeleine

Meaning: **from the Hebrew, "of Magdala"**

Variations: Madelon, Maud, Madeline, Magda, Magdalene, Malina, Maddy, Lena

Although there are three beatified Magdalenas and a St. Magdalene (or Madeleine), the inspiration for this popular name is, of course, Mary of Magdala. She was not the prostitute who anointed Jesus' feet in Luke's Gospel (7:37-50) or Mary of Bethany, the sister of Martha (*see* p. 69) and Lazarus. What is written of her is that she had "seven devils," and that after her healing by Jesus she became one of his followers. Not only did she wait at the foot of the cross with Mary and the other women, but it was she to whom the risen Christ first appeared; it was also to her that the news of the resurrection was first entrusted. This meant that Mary Magdalene was often known as the "first apostle." In the West, where she was believed to have been both the penitent prostitute and the contemplative Mary of Bethany, she became one of the most loved and revered saints of the Middle Ages.

Feast day: July 22

Symbols: fine clothes and loose hair; a pot of ointment; a skull; a vase; a crucifix

Patron: of penitents, perfumers, hairdressers, glovers, and contemplatives

St. Margaret

Meaning: **from the Greek, "a pearl"**

Variations: Madge, Maggie, Maisie, Mamie, Margaretta, Margery, Marghanita, Margot, Marguerite, Marina, Marjorie, Marjory, May, Meg, Megan, Meghan, Daisy, Greta, Peggy, Rita

Perhaps the most attractive St. Margaret was the gentle and strong-willed English woman of noble birth who escaped to Scotland after William the Conqueror defeated the English royal house. She married Malcolm, the rather brutal king of Scotland, and bore him several children. Her personal influence affected the Scottish court for good, and she also persuaded the church to conform to Western disciplines. She and her husband founded Dunfermline Abbey and one of her sons, David, was to become both a king and a saint. Her feast day is on November 16 and she is a patron of Scotland.

Better known is St. Margaret of Antioch, although the legend of her martyrdom is probably a romantic tale very similar to that of Catherine (*see* p. 18), and she is no longer listed in the Roman Martyrology.

St. Margaret-Mary Alacoque is most well known among Catholics as the seventeenth-century French nun of the Visitation order who had visions of Jesus showing his Sacred Heart. She was directed to spread the practice of particular devotion to the Sacred Heart which, after some opposition from her convent, she did. Her symbol is the Sacred Heart of Jesus shown as a heart in flames, and her feast day is October 16.

St. Mark

Meaning: **from the Latin, "of Mars"—the Roman god of war**

Male variations: Marc, Marcel, Marcus, Marius, Martin

Female variations: Marcella, Marceline, Marcia, Marsha, Martina

If the young man who—wrapped only in a sheet—stole after Jesus and his disciples to the garden of Gethsemane is the author of Mark's Gospel and also Paul's companion and Peter's amanuensis, we can build up a surprisingly full picture of St. Mark. He was probably too young to have been allowed to join Jesus' followers but was obviously drawn to this great teacher.

Despite his symbol being a winged lion, however, Mark was perhaps as nervous as the rest of us. As well as running away from the soldiers in the garden on that fateful night, leaving the only thing he was wearing in their hands, he abandoned Paul on his first missionary journey, being rather overwhelmed by it all. It took all the persuasion of his cousin Barnabas, who was with them, to reconcile Paul to Mark. Still, Mark did recover his courage—and it is a braver person who conquers fear than feels none—and joined Paul again. He accompanied him to Rome where he wrote what is probably the first Gospel. Many scholars believe that this was the memoir of Peter, although it has far more to it than that since it is so cleverly constructed to give the gospel message "between the lines." We do not know what became of Mark after Peter and Paul were executed. It is said that he became bishop of Alexandria and was martyred there and that his body was moved to Venice in the ninth century.

Feast day: April 25

Symbols: a pen; a book and scroll; a winged lion; a scroll with the words *Pax tibi* (Peace be to you)

Patron: of cattle farmers, lawyers, glaziers, and Venice

St. Martha

Meaning: **from the Hebrew, "a lady"**

Variations: Marta, Martie, Marty

Martha is the patron saint of all those people who have little imagination and no great religious feeling but who nevertheless get on with serving other people for the sake of Christ. When Jesus was staying with her family in Bethany, she complained to him that her sister Mary was doing nothing (apart from listening to Jesus) and that she, Martha, was having to do all the cooking on her own; Jesus was unimpressed. He was not about to banish Mary, who was listening so intently, to the kitchen. But it was for Martha that he undertook the dangerous journey back to Bethany when he heard that their brother, Lazarus, had died, and for her that he raised Lazarus from death. Their encounter—"I am the resurrection and the life," "I believe that you are the Messiah, the Son of God" (John 11:25, 27)—is one of the most moving in John's Gospel. It is a little passion, prefiguring Jesus' own, and it is the sensible, grumpy Martha, not the saintly Mary, whose faith evokes Jesus' power. Martha, her sister, and brother are celebrated on the same day.

Feast day: July 29

Symbols: a water pot and asperge; cooking pots; a ladle; a broom; a bunch of keys at her waist; a dragon bound with a girdle

Patron: of housewives, cooks, waiters, and dieticians

St. Martina & St. Martin

Meaning: from the Latin, "of Mars"—the Roman god of war

Female variations: Marta, Martie, Martina, Tina

Male variation: Marty

Women may be named after St. Martina, a legendary Roman martyr, but it is more likely that they would be under the patronage of St. Martin of Tours (born 315), who was one of the most popular saints of the Middle Ages. Many English churches are dedicated to this saint, and the name was given to boys and girls alike (as was common in medieval times), as well as to the bird.

The story most often recounted about Martin, a Hungarian soldier, concerns his time in the Roman army. One day, when he was stationed in Amiens, France, he met a beggar and having nothing to give him, he slashed his cloak in half and shared it with him. Later, Christ, wrapped in the half-cloak, appeared to him in a dream and Martin was converted. He obtained a discharge from the army, not without difficulty, and became a hermit. He then became a monk under St. Hilary and eventually founded his own community.

He was not allowed to live peacefully as a religious for long, however, before the people of Tours insisted that he be consecrated as their bishop. Martin was even more horrified than the other bishops who thought him rather too ascetic and unkempt to do honor to the position. He tried to run away but was betrayed by the loud honking of a goose that he disturbed. As a bishop, Martin continued to travel to the remotest places, preaching and working miracles. At his funeral procession (made up of 2000 monks) there was an outbreak of summer weather; today, good weather at about that time of year is called St. Martin's Summer. His death coincided with the tasting of the new season's wine, so we also use the phrase "Martin-drunk."

Feast day: November 11

Symbols: a horse; a sword and a cloak cut in half; a goose; a scourge; a hare; broken idols; a chair in flames; a demon at his feet

Patron: of beggars, soldiers (especially cavalry), riders, tailors, drinkers, and innkeepers

St. Mary

Meaning: **perhaps from the Egyptian, "beloved"**

Variations: Maia, Maire, Mame, Mamie, Manon, Maria, Marian, Mariana, Marianne, Marice, Marie, Mariel, Marietta, Marilyn,

Marion, Marisa, Maryanne, Masha, Maura, Maureen, May, Meriel, Meryl, Mimi, Minette, Minnie, Miriam, Mitzi, Moira, Moire, Mollie, Molly

Mary, the mother of Christ, is the most revered saint in the Christian world and has several festivals in the church's year. It is not surprising that her name has been one of the most popular for girls in all countries, as well as being used by boys in combination with a masculine name in several countries (like José Maria or Jean-Marie, for example). Mary also has various titles such as María de la Concepción or María del Pilar, the title often being used as a name on its own—so you have girls named Pilar, Concepción, Dolores, Consuela, and Mercedes. The important quality of Mary was her willing obedience to Gabriel's announcements of the divine *fiat*. Her own *fiat* ("let it be with me according to your word") is often seen as the turning point when salvation came to the human race. She is also loved as the faithful woman who carried, bore, and tended Jesus and who witnessed his death.

Principal feast days: December 8, the Immaculate Conception; March 25, the Annunciation; May 31, the Visitation; August 15, her Assumption into heaven; September 8, her birthday; January 1, Mary, Mother of God

Symbols: roses; lilies; the Christ-child

Patron: of all women, especially mothers

St. Matilda

Meaning: from Old German, "battle strength"

Variations: Mattie, Maud, Maude

Matilda was a German queen, the wife of Henry I and mother of Emperor Otto I, Henry the Quarrelsome, St. Bruno, archbishop of

Cologne, and others. After the death of her husband, she lived for another 32 years at the mercy of Otto and Henry's unkindness. Her compassion for the poor and her devotion to the church particularly annoyed them, but it earned her, at the very least, the love of her people.

Feast day: March 14

Symbols: a church and crucifix; a money bag; an altar

St. Matthew

Meaning: **from the Hebrew, "gift of God"**

Male variations: Matt, Matthias

Female variations: Mattea, Matthea, Mattie, Matty

Surprisingly little is known about the man who gave us the longest of the Synoptic Gospels. Matthew appears in his Gospel as a Jew who was collaborating with Romans as one of their tax collectors. He may be the Levi, also a tax collector, in Mark and Luke. Jesus' call to follow him must have surprised the other disciples since "good" Jews hated the collaborators, but he is said to have obeyed the call at once, leaving his ill-gotten gains for a rather more ascetic lifestyle. Tradition has it that Matthew was martyred in Ethiopia or Persia and that his remains were brought to Brittany, France.

Feast day: September 21

Symbols: a money bag or a chest; a winged man; a dolphin; a scroll of his Gospel; a carpenter's square; an axe; pen and ink; a sword; stones

Patron: of all who work with money, including, of course, tax men and tax women

St. Maximilian

Meaning: **from the Latin, "the greatest"**

Male variations: Max, Maxime, Maximus

Female variation: Maxine

The Second World War witnessed the death of many Christians, some of whom showed a depth of faith which still inspires people today. One of these was Maximilian Kolbe, who was executed in 1941 and canonized in 1983. Fr. Maximilian Kolbe was a Polish Franciscan friar who became the head of a large friary at Niepokalonow. With great courage, the friars sheltered many refugees, many of whom were Jewish. Maximilian was arrested and taken to Auschwitz. He worked ceaselessly to encourage and support his fellow friars and the other prisoners, and when one was arbitrarily chosen to suffer death by starvation as a reprisal for another prisoner's escape, Fr. Kolbe offered to take his place. He remained as cheerful and calm as ever for a fortnight, always encouraging the men who were suffering and dying alongside him. Eventually, the Nazis lost patience and gave him a lethal injection on August 14.

Feast day: August 14

Patron: of all those who have become dependent on drugs

St. Melania

Meaning: **from the Greek, "black-haired"**

Variations: Mel, Mela, Melanie, Melinda, Melly, Melony, Lin, Linda, Lynda

There were two St. Melanias, known as the Elder and the Younger, and they were related as grandmother and granddaughter. Melanie the Elder took advantage of her very early widowhood to travel to Palestine and work with St. Jerome in the 370s. She died in Jerusalem in 410, and her feast day is June 8. Her son obviously did not share his mother's spiritual ambitions, for he insisted on marrying off his daughter, Melania the Younger, to a wealthy young cousin called Valerius Pinianus.

Melania's piety and compassion for the poor were an irritation to her family—especially her husband—but after the death of their two babies, he came round to her point of view. They sold much of their property and freed their slaves, much to their family's horror. When Rome was invaded by the Visigoths, however, they were free to escape to North Africa, where Melania had other estates. Later, she and her husband moved to Palestine; after his death, Melania founded a convent on the Mount of Olives where she copied manuscripts until she died in 439. Although she found her grandmother rather a formidable woman, Melania came to know St. Paulinus of Nola, St. Augustine of Hippo, and St. Jerome, and they in turn thought very highly of her and her husband. Theirs is one of the happier stories of a Christian couple in the early church.

Feast day: December 31

Symbols: a model of a church; an open purse

St. Michael

Meaning: **from the Hebrew, "who is like God"**

Male variations: Micah, Michel, Miguel, Mick, Micky, Mike, Mischa, Mitch, Mitchell

Female variations: Michaela, Michele, Michelle, Micheline, Mickie

It may seem strange to venerate an archangel along with once-mortal saints, but Michael has always been a popular "saint." Very many churches are dedicated to him, especially those on hills since a vision of him was seen on Monte Gargano in Italy between 492 and 496. It is not only in the Christian calendar that Michael is so important; he is also honored by Jews and Muslims as one of God's greatest angels and captain of the heavenly host, continually fighting the devil (or his human representatives). The association of Michael with fighting comes from the verses in Revelation (12:7-9) about the great war in heaven, but he is also considered to be a special protector of the sick in the Eastern Orthodox Church. There is a tradition which says that Michael receives dying souls and weighs them in his scales, hence his patronage of grocers.

Feast day: September 29

Symbols: a man in full armor and with huge wings, often carrying a shield and scales

Patron: of grocers and supermarket staff, soldiers, radiologists, and the dying

St. Monica

Meaning: **unknown**

Female variations: Mona, Monique

Monica, in these days of an awareness of psychology, has suffered a bad press. The woman who literally pursued her son to urge his conversion and baptism is often thought of nowadays as just another manipulative and domineering mother. In fact, she produced one of the most brilliant theologians and writers of the ancient or modern eras, whose autobiography speaks of her with great affection—so she must have done something right! The son, of course, was Augustine (354–430), who was born in Thagaste, North Africa, and who returned from his studies under St. Ambrose in Italy to become the bishop of Hippo in 396. Monica never saw his consecration, for she died at the Italian port of Ostia on their journey back to

Africa. One of the most moving chapters of Augustine's *Confessions* records their almost ecstatic conversation about heaven together there, one night, looking over the sea. Monica died about five days later.

Feast day: August 27

Symbols: a monstrance; a veil or handkerchief; a book; a girdle; a staff

Patron: of mothers

St. Mungo

Meaning: **from the Gaelic, "darling"**

Mungo, in fact, is the nickname of Bishop Kentigern, who is thought to have founded the church at Glasgow and who died c. 612. There are stories of him being forced to flee to Wales, where he was able to found a monastery. St. Asaph succeeded Kentigern as abbot when the latter returned to Scotland by order of King Rederech, who was a Christian. No one knows the truth of all this nor of the extraordinary miracles attributed to him, but the emblems of one of them—a ring and a fish—are on the heraldic arms of Glasgow city, of which he is patron.

The story goes that the queen gave a ring, which had been her husband's present to her, to a knight of his court with whom she was in love. While the king and the knight were out hunting one day, they rested by a river. The knight fell asleep and the king noticed the ring on his finger. Suppressing his rage, he slipped the ring off and threw it into the river, saying nothing. When he returned home, however, he demanded the ring of his wife and, when she could not produce it, ordered her execution. She could get no help from the knight, so she begged help from St. Kentigern. He was filled with pity for her since his own mother, a Pictish princess, had been seduced by Eugenius III, king of the Scots. So he prayed that the woman would be granted time for repentance. The ring was miraculously recovered from the belly of a salmon caught in the Clyde, and the queen lived to do penance and to become a faithful wife.

Feast day: January 14

Symbols: a ring and a fish

N

St. Natalia

Meaning: from the Latin, "the birth" (that is, of Christ)

Variations: Natalie, Nathalia, Nathalie, Natasha, Natty, Nettie, Tasha

Two Natalias are venerated as martyrs, together with their husbands. Nothing much is known of the ninth-century Natalia and Aurelius except that they were beheaded in Toledo during the Moorish persecutions. Their feast day is July 27.

The earlier Natalia is thought, in fact, to have died in peace long after witnessing the cruel execution of Adrian, her husband. He was one of the pagan officers in Nicomedia and was so impressed by the courage of the Christian prisoners in his charge that he became a Christian himself, inevitably ending up in his own jail. Natalia did all she could to alleviate the Christians' sufferings, but she could not prevent their deaths at the stake. A great storm quenched the fires before the bodies were burned, and Natalia—along with some of the Christian community—took the remains of these martyrs to be buried at Argyropolis. She remained there until her death when she was buried alongside them.

Feast day: August 26

Symbols: an anvil; a lion; a tomb

St. Nathanael

Meaning: from the Hebrew, "God has given"

Variations: Nat, Nathan, Nathaniel, Natty

See St. Bartholomew, page 12.

St. Nicholas

Meaning: from the Greek, "victory of the people"

Male variations: Nick, Nicky, Nichol, Claus, Cole, Colet, Colin

Female variations: Nicola, Nicole, Nicolette, Colette

St. Nicholas is one of the most popular saints as can be seen by the number of other saints who share his name and the many variants of it for both boys and girls. He is, of course, better known as Father Christmas or Santa Claus. In many northern European countries, he fills shoes or stockings on December 6, rather than on Christmas Eve.

We only know for certain that he was the bishop of Myra, in Asia Minor, in the fourth century. The popular legend that he saved three sisters from remaining unmarried (or worse) by throwing three bags of gold through their window, thus rendering them rich and marriageable, made the link with an anonymous bringer of presents. Apparently, a picture of this story was so confusing that it was understood to be Nicholas bringing back to life three children who had been murdered and hidden in a pickle tub, so the bishop developed a reputation for being especially fond of children. He was also credited with the rescue of shipwrecked sailors and three prisoners condemned to death.

Brewer's *Dictionary of Phrase and Fable* suggests that the reason the Knights of St. Nicholas is another name for thieves is not because Nicholas aids and abets them but because he once induced some to give back what they had stolen. It is also reassuring to know that Old Nick as a name for the devil has nothing to do with the good bishop, but comes from Nick—a Scandinavian evil spirit.

Feast day: December 6

Symbols: three golden apples on a book; three purses; three loaves; three golden apples; an anchor; a ship; a Trinity symbol on a cope (ceremonial cloak)

Patron: of children (especially boys), sailors, pawnbrokers, merchants, captives, Russia, and many other places and churches

O

St. Olivia & St. Oliver

Meaning: **from the Latin, "olive tree"**

Female variations: Olive, Olivette, Ollie, Olva, Liva, Livia, Livy, Nola, Nollie,

Male variations: Ollie, Noll

No one is sure if the story of the beautiful Christian girl from Palermo who was carried away by pirates to Tunis is true. Once there, she lived the life of a hermit, but so many Muslims were converted by her example of holiness and her power to work miracles that the authorities tortured and executed her. What is certain is that she is, perhaps oddly, venerated among Muslims of Tunis even today, and the mosque of the city is called Temple of Olive. Her feast day is June 10, and she is often portrayed in art with a brazier and leaden ropes.

Oliver Plunket was the last Catholic martyr to be hung, drawn, and quartered at Tyburn in 1681. He was born in Ireland in 1629 and became bishop of Armargh at the age of 40. He set about reforming the church while trying to maintain good relations with the Protestant bishops, but the political troubles in Ireland overwhelmed Christian principles. He was betrayed, tried and released, and then tried again—this time in London—where a corrupt court found him guilty and sentenced him to death. His feast day is July 1.

P

St. Patrick

Meaning: from the Latin, "of the noble patrician class"

Male variations: Paddie, Paddy, Padraic, Padraig, Pat, Patrice

Female variations: Paddie, Pat, Patrice, Patricia, Patsy, Pattie, Tricia, Trish, Trisha

St. Patrick has become synonymous with Ireland, the land to which he came as a missionary bishop in 432. It is rather surprising considering that Patrick was not Irish but a Romano-Briton and his first experience of Ireland was as a slave when he was captured and sold into slavery for about six years. After escaping to France and being consecrated by St. Germanus in Auxerre, Patrick returned to Ireland, where he traveled about, teaching and working miracles as well as writing.

One of his best-loved traits was that of teaching the truths of the faith using homely, simple images; his example of the shamrock (or cloverleaf) representing the mystery of the Trinity has become universal as well as his own personal symbol. He founded the great church at Armargh in 444 (where Oliver Plunket became bishop over 1000 years later) and died in 461.

Feast day: March 17

Symbols: an archbishop's cross; a shamrock; an Irish harp; fire; a font; a miter; a dragon; a long staff; a wallet

Patron: of Ireland and Nigeria

St. Paul

Meaning: from the Latin, "small"

Variations: Paulinus, Pablo, Pauly

St. Paul needs no introduction. He was the apostle who first took the gospel to the Gentile world and who wrote many of the letters in the New Testament. He is also one of the apostles Luke writes about in Acts and is believed to have been martyred in Rome during Nero's persecution of Christians, around 68. Many other St. Pauls have followed, from Cyprus, Italy, Japan, Korea, and even Roman Britain. The original St. Paul seems to have been intellectually brilliant, something of a mystic, an indefatigable traveler, and at times hot tempered.

Feast day: June 29 and January 25

Symbols: a book and sword; a serpent and fire; a palm tree; three fountains; a phoenix; scrolls with the names of his epistles

Patron: of tentmakers (his own trade) and upholsterers

St. Paula

Variations: Pauline Paulette

St. Paula of Bethlehem (347–404) was a Roman noblewoman who married and had five children. When her husband died, she became a disciple of St. Jerome and with her daughter, St. Eustochium, founded a convent and a pilgrim's hospice in Bethlehem. By all accounts, she was also intellectually gifted, learning both Greek and Hebrew and studying the Bible. Jerome's letters praise her practical efficiency and her diplomacy but are concerned about her excessive self-discipline and generosity to others. There is another St. Paula, of the nineteenth century, three other beatified Paulas, and a

Blessed Pauline, a German woman, who founded the Sisters of Christian Charity in 1849.

Feast day: January 26

Symbols: instruments of the Passion; a book and staff; a sponge; a scourge

Patron: of widows

St. Peter

***Meaning:* from the Greek, "a rock"**

Male variations: Parry, Pearce, Pedro, Perkin, Perry, Pete, Pierce, Piers, Pyrs

Female variations: Peta, Petra, Piera, Petrina, Pierina

Peter was, of course, pre-eminent among the apostles, being not only one of the inner circle of three (together with James and John), but also the disciple to whom Jesus entrusted the Church: "You are Peter, and on this rock I will build my church" (Matt 16:18).

From the Gospels, we have a picture of a fisherman who lived with his wife in Galilee and fished with his brother, Andrew, until they were called by Jesus to become fishers of people. He was the apostle who denied his master three times on the night of Jesus' betrayal and yet he was the man whom the risen Jesus told to "feed my lambs" (John 21:15). He traveled to Rome, where he became the leader of the Church, and it is thought that he dictated his memories to Mark, forming the first Gospel. And it was there that he faced execution, together with Paul, in about 67. There are legends of him traveling to Antioch with his wife and daughter, Petronilla (whose name, incidentally, is not derived from Peter, as many think, but from the Latin, Petronius)—but these are probably legendary.

Feast day: June 29

Symbols: two crossed keys; a crowing cock; a fish; two swords; a shepherd's staff and two keys

Patron: of fishers, boat builders, and clockmakers

St. Philip

Meaning: from the Greek, "a lover of horses"

Male variations: Felipe, Phil, Pip

Female variations: Philippa, Phili, Pippa, Pippi

Philip was another of the 12 apostles who lived in Bethsaida in Galilee until he was called to follow Jesus. We know much less about him than Peter, but he was one of the disciples at the feeding of the 5000, so bread has become one of his symbols in art. The deacon in Acts 8:26-39 who converted Queen Candace's treasurer as he traveled back to Ethiopia after worshiping in Jerusalem is another Philip whose feast is June 6. He also was the first to proclaim the gospel in Samaria. Tradition has it that the apostle went to Phrygia and was martyred at Hieropolis, but this is not known for certain.

Feast day: May 3

Symbols: a basket; three loaves and a cross; a carpenter's square; a patriarchal cross and spear

Patron: of Luxembourg and Uruguay

Q

St. Quentin

Meaning: **from the Latin, "a fifth child," or after the Roman tribe of the Quintii**

Male variations: Quinn, Quint, Quintin, Quinton

Female variations: Quinta, Quintilla

St. Quentin was martyred sometime around 300 in the French town that bears his name, although nothing certain about him is known. Some think that he was the son of a Roman senator and was an officer in the Roman army before forsaking his wealth and position to become a missionary to Gaul. The symbols associated with him all refer to the many tortures he was said to have suffered, but why he is patron of bombardiers, chaplains, locksmiths, tailors, and porters is a mystery. Perhaps he should be a patron of all prisoners, for it is said that he was once released from prison by an angel.

Feast day: October 31

Symbols: a broken wheel; iron spits; an x-shaped cross

R

St. Raymond

Meaning: **from the Old German, "strong or wise defense"**

Male variations: Ramon, Ray, Raymund

Female variations: Ramona, Raymonda, Raymonde

St. Raymond of Peñafort (January 7) and St. Peter Nolasco cofounded the order of Our Lady of Ransom or the Mercedarians in the early thirteenth century. This was a Spanish order dedicated to rescuing Christians who had been taken prisoner by the Moorish occupation. St. Raymond Nonnatus joined the order and went to Algeria with ransom money for prisoners. When the money ran out, he offered himself in exchange for another man. This was agreed, but the Moors had not perhaps reckoned with Raymond's determination to preach the gospel, even in their own territory. Threatened by the flow of converts and determined to stop him, they found an effective but crude method: they put a padlock through his lips and put him into prison. His guards were either kinder or greedier. They kept Raymond alive, at any rate, until he was himself ransomed by the order and was able to make the journey home, where he died in 1240. His nickname means "not born," which refers to the story that his mother died in childbirth. Raymond was delivered from her body by a doctor, and he is thought to have a special concern for "all women laboring of child."

Feast day: August 31

Symbols: a padlock; three or four crowns; a crown of thorns

Patron: of pregnant women and babies, midwives and obstetricians, and Catalonia

St. Richard

Meaning: **from Old English, "a strong ruler"**

Male variations: Richie, Rick, Ricky, Ritchie, Ricardo, Dick, Dickon

Female variations: Richarda, Richenda, Rickie, Ricky

To drop the chalice during Mass must be every priest's nightmare, but St. Richard of Chichester once did and apparently he miraculously did not spill a drop. Richard was born in 1197 and studied at Oxford, Paris, and Bologna. He became the chancellor of Oxford University and later served as chancellor to St. Edmund of Abingdon, who was then the archbishop of Canterbury. Trouble began when St. Boniface of Mainz and King Henry III quarreled over the right of appointment to the see of Chichester. Boniface appointed Richard, known to be a strong-minded and ascetic pastor as well as a scholar, whereas Henry had his own favorite, one of his own court who was, nevertheless, "deficient in learning." Richard had to wait for two years before the pope upheld his claim, but once he took possession of his see, he proved to be a very effective and much-loved bishop.

Feast day: April 3

Symbols: a plow; a book and staff; a chalice at his feet

Patron: of coach drivers

St. Robert

Meaning: from Old German, "bright fame"

Male variations: Rab, Rabbie, Rob, Robbie, Robby, Roberto, Robin, Rupert, Bert, Bertie, Bob, Bobbie

Female variations: Robbie, Robena, Roberta, Robin, Robina, Ruperta, Bobbie

There is a melancholy list of Roberts among the English Catholic martyrs of the Reformation, of whom the poet Robert Southwell (February 21) is the most famous, but there are the happier lives of St. Robert of Molesme and St. Robert Bellarmine to recount.

St. Robert of Molesme was an eleventh-century monk who founded a monastery at Molesme in Burgundy but who eventually became one of the co-founders of the great Cistercian monastery at Citeaux. He was the abbot there for 18 months but then returned to Molesme, where he ruled as abbot until his death at the age of 84. His feast is celebrated on April 29.

Robert Bellarmine was one of the greatest Jesuit scholars of the Renaissance and may take some credit for being sympathetic to (although not completely persuaded by) Galileo during the scientist's persecution by the church. His feast day is September 17, and he is patron of all ecclesiastical lawyers and catechists.

St. Rock

Meaning: from Old German, "crow," or Old English, "rock"

St. Rock (or Roch) was well known and loved in France and Italy as a healer of disease, especially contagious diseases. He was born in 1293 to the wealthy governor of Montpellier. His parents died when he was still a young man, and Rock gave away all his wealth in order to become a pilgrim. On his way to Rome, he healed many people of the plague, which was then raging in Italy, until he himself became infected. He went into the forest to die, but was cared for by a dog who brought him food, and there the saint recovered. Rock returned to Montpellier so starved and looking so ill that none of his family recognized him and he was arrested as an imposter. For five years he lay in prison. When he died, it was discovered that he had the same birthmark as the infant Rock: the mark of a cross on his chest.

Feast day: August 16

Symbol: a dog

Patron: of healers, prisoners, and dog owners

St. Rose

Meaning: **from the Latin, "rose"**

Variations: Rhoda, Rois, Rosa, Rosetta, Rosie, Rosina, Rosita, Roslyn, Rosy

St. Rose of Lima (1586–1617) was the first American-born person to be canonized although she was the daughter of Spanish parents who had come to settle in Peru. She was born in Lima and became a Dominican tertiary at the age of 20. Although she led an outwardly simple life, growing flowers and doing embroidery in order to help the family's finances, Rose inflicted terrible tortures on herself for fear of vanity and seemed to endure strange mystical experiences, which were investigated by the church. Nowadays these are often considered to be signs of psychiatric disorder rather than holiness. Nevertheless, Rose was canonized not for these self-destructive traits but for her sympathy for the poor and slaves, the sick and the Peruvian Indians.

Feast day: August 23

Symbols: a crown of roses and thorns; a needle and thimble;
a spiked crown

Patron: of florists and gardeners, Latin America, the Philippines,
and Peru

St. Rupert

Meaning: **from Old German, "bright fame"**

Female variation: Ruperta

One St. Rupert (together with his mother, St. Bertha) lived as a
hermit on the Rupertsburg near Bingen in the ninth century and
became particularly well loved by the much more famous Hildegard of Bingen when she was abbess there 300 years later. His feast
day is April 15. Another St. Rupert, who has been particularly popular in Ireland, was a Frenchman of the seventh century who became bishop of Worms. He later became a missionary to Bavaria
and then to Austria.

Feast day: March 27

Symbols: a salt box; a model of a church; a basket of eggs

S

St. Simon

Meaning: **from the Hebrew, "God has heard," or from the Greek, "snub-nosed"**

Male variations: Si, Sim, Simeon

Female variation: Simone

As one of the Twelve, Simon the Zealot is one of the foremost saints in the Christian calendar; as one of the most anonymous, nothing much is known about him. The nickname Zealot suggests that he was one of the underground Jewish freedom fighters who risked death by crucifixion for their terrorist warfare against the occupying Roman forces. Some traditions say that after the resurrection he went to Egypt and Persia and was later martyred, and he is often venerated together with St. Jude. Their feast day is October 28, and Simon is often portrayed with the symbols of a fish and book, two fishes, an oar, a ship, or a fuller's bat.

An English saint, Simon Stock, was born in Kent in 1165 and became the prior general of the Carmelites. Under his able leadership, four new houses were opened in the great medieval university cities of Oxford, Cambridge, Paris, and Bologna. Carmelites wear a scapular—a long, wide band of cloth, with a hole for the head, worn over the habit—and Simon once had a vision of Mary who told him that no one who wore the scapular would ever go to hell. This is the origin of the widespread sale of tiny token scapulars often worn by Roman Catholics—but whether this is quite what Mary had in mind is not clear. St. Simon died in 1265 at Bordeaux but his body was brought back to be buried in Aylesford in Kent.

Feast day: May 16

Patron: of leatherworkers

St. Sophia

Meaning: **from the Greek, "wisdom"**

Variations: Sonia, Sonnie, Sonya, Sophie

Although Sophie or Sophia has become a popular name, the saints who bore it are generally forgotten or legendary, like the martyr who is supposed to have been the mother of St. Faith and her sisters. Perhaps it is the meaning of the name, "wisdom," which has brought it back into fashion.

The most famous St. Sophie is St. Madeleine Sophie Barat, who was born in Joigny, France, in 1779. Her brother, who was 11 years older, was her godfather and undertook her education when she was 10 in Latin, Greek, history, physics, and mathematics. From the age of 15 on, the Bible, the Fathers of the Church, and theology were her main subjects. In 1800, she and three companions began the Society of the Sacred Heart. She became the superior in 1802, an office she held for 63 years. She died in 1865. Her feast day is May 25.

St. Stephen

Meaning: **from the Greek, "crowned"**

Male variations: Steffan, Stephan, Steve, Steven, Stevie, Esteban

Female variations: Stephanie, Steffie, Steph, Stephana, Steve, Stevie

St. Stephen is, of course, in the Christmas carol "Good King Wenceslas." The story of his death is written in Acts 6–7, and it tells of how Stephen, who had been chosen by the community as one of the band of seven deacons and may have been their head, "did great wonders and signs" and became a powerful preacher.

Some angry Jews who were affronted by the claims of the disciples brought him before the council and accused him of blasphemy. He addressed the council with the sermon recorded in Acts (which is, indeed, stirring stuff!); as he finished, he exclaimed in wonder at the vision he had, "I see the heavens opened and the Son of Man standing at the right hand of God." The crowd stoned Stephen to death for blasphemy, according to Jewish law. Like his Lord, Stephen gave his soul to God as he died and prayed that his executioners would not be found guilty of their sin.

Feast day: December 26

Symbols: a dalmatic (the tunic worn by deacons); three stones; stones in a napkin; stones on a book

Patron: of stonemasons, builders, and horses

St. Susanna

Meaning: **from the Hebrew, "lily"**

Variations: Shushana, Susan, Sosanna, Sue, Sukey, Suki, Susanne, Susie, Suzanna, Suzanne, Suzette, Suzi, Zsa-Zsa

One St. Susanna may have been the beautiful niece of St. Caius, bishop of Rome, who was sought after by the Emperor Diocletian's friend, Maximian. When she refused him, she, her father, and two uncles were all executed. Whatever the truth of the story, there was a Susanna who was martyred and buried in Rome. The popularity of this name is perhaps due more to the heroine in the biblical book of Tobit, but there are several saints called Susanna, including another martyr from Armenia who married a Russian prince from Georgia and who was killed by Persians in 473.

Feast day: August 11

Symbols: a crown at her feet, a sword

St. Teresa

Meaning: **from the Greek, "of Tharasia" or "reaper"**

Female variations: Terese, Terrie, Terry, Tess, Tessa, Theresa, Therese, Theresia, Tracey, Tracy

St. Teresa of Avila and St. Thérèse of Lisieux are two of the most extraordinary women of the church, and both of them were quite different.

Teresa was a witty, energetic woman of the world who nevertheless became one of the greatest contemplatives. She worked with St. John of the Cross and others to reform the Carmelite Order, in which she had become professed as a nun. She lived during the time of the Counter-Reformation in Spain when there was a great flowering of learning and discipline in the Roman Catholic Church amidst the careless laxity of many of the clergy and religious houses. Certainly, much of that flowering is to Teresa's credit, and she was the first woman to be honored as a Doctor of the Church for all her writings on prayer and the inner life.

Conversely, her letters and the descriptions of her that survive show us a fascinatingly contradictory saint who was impatient with "stupid nuns" and yet humble about her own intellectual abilities; an ecstatic visionary who distrusted the supernatural phenomena which occurred around her; a brilliant cook; and someone who was determined to lead those who would follow her into a life of strict austerity and discipline.

Feast day: October 15

Symbols: roses and lilies; a heart in flames; flaming arrows; a dove

Patron: of Spain

Thérèse, by contrast, was a young and simple nineteenth-century Frenchwoman who died of tuberculosis at the age of 24. Opinions about her differ: to many thousands, her autobiography, *The Story of a Soul,* is a work of spiritual genius in its simplicity, humility, and ordinariness. (She is patron of missionaries and ship pilots because she would offer to God, on their behalf, the few painful steps she was able to make each day during her illness.) Her powers of intercession were and are believed to be miraculous, and the shrine at Lisieux is one of the largest in the Roman Catholic Church. To others, the Little Flower—as she liked to call herself—was a nauseating product of a rather febrile kind of French spirituality.

St. Teresa and St. Thérèse speak to different kinds of people, but they both experienced the love of God intensely and could communicate the depths of their experience to others—that, not their brand of spirituality, is what matters.

Feast day: October 1

Symbol: flowers

Patron: of florists, missionaries, airline pilots, and France

St. Thomas

Meaning: **from the Aramaic, "a twin"**

Male variations: Tam, Tamas, Tom, Tomás, Tompkin, Tommy

Female variations: Tamsin, Tamasine, Thomasina, Tammy, Tamara

Many St. Thomases take their name from the apostle who is often called Doubting Thomas from the story in John's Gospel (20:24-29). John also recalls him as the apostle of the heroic or fatalistic comment in 11:16—"Let us also go, that we may die with him"—

when Jesus was preparing to go to Bethany, where Lazarus had died. It is also John who calls him Didymus or the twin although we do not know who his twin was. Thomas' recognition of the risen Christ ("My Lord and my God!" John 20:28) has become a powerful meditation prayer for many Christians. That is as much as we know of Thomas, the apostle, although a much later book called the *Acts of Thomas* (written in the second and fourth centuries by members of sects such as the Gnostics) describes his founding of the church in Kerala in southern India.

Feast day: July 3

Symbols: a spear and lance; a carpenter's square and lance; a builder's rule; the five wounds of Christ; the Virgin Mary's girdle; a book and spear

Patron: of architects, builders, carpenters, masons, and surveyors

Thomas à Becket (1118–1170), the statesman and archbishop of Canterbury who was murdered by Henry II, was the most important English saint in the Middle Ages, and his shrine became the most important center for pilgrims after Rome and Santiago de Compostela. Although he was clearly similar to a politician in his obstinacy and ambition, he took his consecration as archbishop very seriously and became known for his devotion, austerity, and defense of the church against the king. His feast day is December 29 and his help is invoked for blindness.

Thomas More (1478–1535), who was beheaded by Henry VIII, also refused to compromise his Christian beliefs for political expediency. He is another English saint loved for his wide learning and humanity; his feast is June 22. He is the patron of civil servants and lawyers.

The other very well known St. Thomas is, of course, the great theologian St. Thomas Aquinas (1225–1274), whose symbol is a star and who was himself the star of medieval science, theology, and prayer. Naturally, he is the patron of scholars, especially theologians. It is reasonable, therefore, that he should also be the patron of all pencil makers. His feast is celebrated January 28.

St. Timothy

Meaning: **from the Greek, "honor to God"**

Male variations: Tim, Timmie, Timmy

Female variation: Timothea

St. Paul writes to Timothy with such obvious and avuncular affection that it is hard not to feel it too although we know only a little about him. Indeed, Paul ends his second letter to Timothy with a moving appeal for his company. From Acts and Paul's letters we know that he was Jewish through his mother, Eunice, but had a Greek father. Although Eunice and her mother, Lois, were Christians and had brought Timothy up as a Christian too, Paul himself gave Timothy instruction in the faith and also had him circumcised in order to show the Jewish Christians that Christianity was not radically anti-Jewish but a fulfillment of everything they believed in. Later, Timothy was given charge over the church at Ephesus and is thought to have been its first bishop. Some say that he was beaten to death for his opposition to the pagan festivities in honor of the Ephesians' goddess and great tourist attraction, Diana.

Feast day: January 26

Symbols: a club and stones; a broken image of the goddess Diana

Patron: of people with digestive disorders ("Take a little wine for the sake of your stomach," Paul tells him in 1 Tim 5:23)

U

St. Ursula

Meaning: **from the Latin, "little bear"**

Female variations: Orsa, Ulla, Ursa, Ursulina

Male variation: Orson

Apparently, Ursula was a British princess who refused to marry a pagan suitor until, playing for time, she had made a pilgrimage to Rome with 11,000 virgins. The required companions were eventually found and Ursula set off with her entourage to Rome, where she met the pope. She was assured in a dream that she would be martyred on the return journey and would therefore avoid the threat of marriage; she told this to the pope who, also keen for martyrdom, then joined her. When they reached Cologne on the return journey, they met the pagan suitor, who was now converted and also anxious for martyrdom, and there were some Huns who were happy to oblige. Historians believe that some women seem to have been martyred at Cologne before the late fourth century, so maybe this story has a high degree of truth in it. Sadly, Ursula is no longer in the Roman Martyrology, but she has given her name to an order of nuns as well as many other women, and she and her companions are immortalized as "the eleven who went up to heaven" in some interpretations of the song, "Green Grow the Rushes-O." However, the Roman calendar does list other Ursulas, among them St. Ursula Bourla, whose feast day is October 17.

V

St. Valerie

Meaning: **from the Latin, "strong," or from the Roman family name, Valerius**

Female variations: Val, Valeria

Male variations: Val, Valerian, Valery

The most common use of Valerie for English speakers is as a girl's name and must refer back to St. Valeria, who was supposed to have been the wife of St. Vitalis and the mother of St. Gervase and St. Protase. She and her husband are honored as martyrs although nothing is known for certain about them. She and her husband are no longer in the Roman Martyrology. But there are several Valerians who do have feast days.

In France, however, it is St. Walaricus, or St. Valéry, who is honored. Walaricus was a fifth-century monk who began his religious life at Luxeuil and then set out as a missionary to northern France. He later settled down and became an abbot at Leuconaus; he died in 620. It is said that he was specially invoked by William the Conqueror, who wanted fair winds for his foray into England in 1066. Perhaps his obviously efficient intervention in this matter explains why he is still so well thought of on the other side of the English Channel and so obscure to the English. He is remembered on April Fools' Day.

St. Veronica

Meaning: **from the Latin, "a true image"**

Variations: Vera, Verena, Veronique, Nicky, Ronnie

Veronica is an anagram of *vera icon* or "true image," and the name has become associated with the story of the woman of Jerusalem who stopped Jesus on his way to crucifixion and wiped his bloody, perspiring face with her handkerchief. As a miraculous reward for her compassion, Jesus' features were imprinted on the cloth, which is kept as a precious relic in St. Peter's, Rome. Some people believe that Veronica was also the woman with the hemorrhage whom Jesus healed (Mark 5:25-34); others, that the liturgical veil called the vernicle, which had Jesus' head, crowned with thorns, painted on it, eventually became personified as a woman called Veronica. However it may be, Veronica herself has become a true image of compassion in her own right and a beautiful picture in the otherwise brutal story of the crucifixion.

Feast day: July 12

Symbol: Christ's face printed upon a veil

Patron: of laundry workers

St. Victor

Meaning: **from the Latin, "victory"**

Variations: Vic, Vick

There is a second-century martyr called Victor the Moor who was a soldier in the Roman army and supposed to have been beheaded in Milan in 303. Another Victor, of Marseilles (also a soldier in the army), became a Christian and was martyred sometime during the third century. Little is known about him, but the tradition is that he underwent the most frightful tortures, being strengthened by the presence of Christ and hosts of angels. When he was taken to bow down before pagan gods, Victor merely kicked them over and had his foot cut off before he was finally beheaded. These Victors are remembered on May 8 and July 21 respectively.

St. Victoria

Variations: Vicki, Vickie, Vicky, Victorine, Vita

There were three women named Victoria martyred in the early church. One was an African girl who ran away with several other Christians and who chose death with them rather than being married to a pagan or making a plea of insanity. Another was martyred with her sister, Anatolia, in Italy, and another was killed with her husband, Acisclus, in Spain. Their feast days are February 12, July 10, and November 17.

St. Vincent

Meaning: **from the Latin, "conquering"**

Male variations: Vin, Vince, Vincente, Vinny

Female variation: Vincentia

Both of the St. Vincents who are still well known lived up to their name. The first, St. Vincent of Lérins, was a great theologian who retired to the tiny island off Cannes and yet whose work on the Trinity shaped the church's self-understanding even to this day. He was one of the great writers against the Arian heresy and, indeed, many people believe that he or a disciple wrote what we call the

Athanasian Creed. He also gave a usefully elastic definition of what is catholic truth: that is, that it must always have been held to be true, "always, everywhere, and by all the faithful." This definition is still used in ecclesiastical arguments today. His feast day is May 24.

The enemy of St. Vincent de Paul was not so much a theological heresy as a materialistic streak, so it is a remarkable thing that he has become synonymous, in France at least, with the care and service of the poor. Born in 1580 of very poor parents, Vincent seemed to be a "career priest" in the corrupt atmosphere of aristocratic France. What changed his heart may have been his experience of living and working with people who lived in great luxury side by side with others in extreme poverty. Or it may have been the influence of Fr. Berulle and Madame de Gondi, who were working in Paris. Whatever caused him to do it, Vincent founded a congregation dedicated to helping the most destitute in society and encouraged St. Louise de Marillac (*see* p. 64) to begin a similar congregation for women, the Sisters of Charity. He even took the place of a galley-slave for some months, ruining his own health, in order to restore the slave to his family. Throughout his life, he managed to continue his friendship with the rich and influential, even the French queen, Anne of Austria. He encouraged them to use their position to help the poor, while giving himself unreservedly to the most helpless in society.

Feast day: September 27

Symbols: a model of an orphanage or hospital; a child in his arms

Patron: of all charities, hospitals, prisons, and Madagascar

St. William

Meaning: **from Old German, "helmet of resolution"**

Male variations: Will, Willie, Willis, Willy, Wilmot, Wilson, Guillermo, Bill, Billie, Billy, Gwylim, Liam

Female variations: Wilhelmina, Wilella, Wilhelmine, Willa, Willamina, Wilma, Wilmette, Wilmot, Wylma, Billie, Billy, Min, Mina, Minna, Minnie, Valma, Velma, Vilette, Vilma

William is such a popular name that it is hardly surprising that there are many listed in the calendar of saints as well as a sad roll of beatified men who were tortured and executed during the Reformation in England. It is difficult to choose any one of them rather than another, but St. William of Gellone (d. 812) seems to have been an attractive character simply because he combined outward "masculine" virtues, in order to be the ideal Christian knight, with more inward qualities that led him to found an abbey near Aniane, to which he retired as a monk. He is remembered on May 28.

St. William of York was also a rather interesting mixture of the pragmatic and spiritual. He was appointed bishop of York in 1140, but there was a great deal of fuss because his enemies accused him of simony (buying or selling church appointments) and sexual laxity. Pope Innocent II upheld his cause and he was consecrated, but seven years later he was deposed by Pope Eugenius III on the advice of St. Bernard of Clairvaux among others. He must have had redeeming qualities, however, for after spending some years in ascetic seclusion, Pope Anastasius IV restored him to his see, to the joy of his flock. His feast day is June 8.

St. Winifred

Meaning: **from Old German, "peaceful friend," or Old Welsh, "blessed reconciliation"**

Variations: Win, Winnie, Winny, Wyn, Wynne, Freda, Fredi, Freddie, Gwenfrewi

There were many springs associated with healing in medieval Britain, often the origin of a town or village and often called Holywell or having the suffix "well." Holywell in North Wales grew up on the spot where Winifred (Gwenfrewi) was beheaded by the furious and frustrated Caradog of Hawarden, who had wanted to marry this chaste Christian girl. Her uncle, St. Beuno, calmly replaced Winifred's head and thus restored her to life, and Caradog was swallowed up by the earth beneath his feet. Winifred became a nun and died at Gwytherin about 650. The spring became a place of pilgrimage for over 1000 years.

Feast day: November 3

Symbols: a shepherd's staff; a sword

Z

St. Zachary

Meaning: **from the Hebrew, "God has remembered"**

Variations: Zacharias, Zachariah, Zack, Zacky, Zak, Zechariah, Zeke

The story of Zechariah (or Zachary in its popular English form) at the beginning of Luke's Gospel forms a diptych with that of Joseph. He was the father of Jesus' cousin, John the Baptist, and occasionally served as a priest in the Temple. The angel Gabriel (*see* p. 39) appeared to him while he was performing his priestly tasks to announce the conception of John by his wife, Elizabeth, although she was elderly and barren. Zechariah, like his counterpart Joseph, was incredulous at first, so much so that he was silenced for his unbelief. This lasted until the child was born and he had corroborated his wife's obedient decision to name her promised child John, as the angel had directed. If Zechariah was initially faithless, he did eventually catch on. Like Doubting Thomas, Zechariah might be a special patron of the cynical and slow.

Feast day: November 5

Symbols: a thurible; a priest's vestments; an altar; an angel; a lighted candle

St. Zoe

Meaning: **from the Greek, "life"; used to translate Eve from the Hebrew into Greek**

Another martyr of the early church, Zoe was married to a slave called Hesperus and had two children. They were forced by their owners to eat food sacrificed to pagan gods; but when the two children refused and cheerfully put up with the most ferocious tortures under their parents' gaze, Zoe and Hesperus were inspired. Zoe was hung from a tree by her hair and then the whole family was roasted alive for their integrity and faith.

Feast day: May 2

A Calendar of Saints

This is a brief index of days and some of the saints commonly associated with them. All of the saints listed here are in the Roman Martyrology, but calendars differ and have been revised from time to time so some saints may be remembered on different days or may not be celebrated in the United States or Canada. This list, however, should give some inspiration for birthdays and namedays.

January
1 Mary, Mother of God; William of Saint-Bénigne
2 Basil the Great; Gregory Nazianzen
3 Genevieve of Paris; Fintan
4 Elizabeth Bayley Seton; Angela of Foligno
5 John Neumann; Emiliana; Edward the Confessor
6 André Bessette; Raphaela Maria
7 Raymond of Peñafort; Mary-Theresa of the Sacred Heart
8 Lawrence Giustiniani
9 Adrian of Canterbury; Agatha Yi; Teresa Kim
10 Peter Orseolo; Ana of Monteagudo
11 Theodosius of Cathismus; Honorata of Pavia
12 Benedict Biscop; Margaret Bourgeoys
13 Hilary of Poitiers; Veronica of Binasco
14 Felix of Nola; Kentigern (Mungo); Macrina the Elder
15 Paul the Hermit; Ita of Killeedy; Alexander Arnold Janssen
16 Priscilla; Joseph Vaz
17 Anthony of Egypt; Roseline
18 Beatrice d'Este; Margaret of Hungary; James Hilary
19 Macarius the Elder; Henry of Uppsala
20 Sebastian; Fabian
21 Agnes; Zachary the Hermit
22 Vincent of Zaragoza; Laura Vicuña

23 Severinus and Aquila
24 Francis de Sales
25 Paul
26 Paula; Timothy
27 Angela Merici; Maura
28 Thomas Aquinas; Julian of Cuenca
29 Valerius; Villana of Florence
30 Hyacintha Mariscotti; Sebastian Valfré

February

1 Brigid of Kildare; Reginald of Orleans
2 Lawrence of Canterbury; Joan de Lestonnac
3 Blaise; Claudia Thévenet
4 Gilbert of Sempringham; Joan of France; Phileas
5 Agatha
6 Dorothy; Paul Miki; Angelo of Furcio
7 Luke the Younger; Juliana of Bologna; Giles Mary
8 Jerome Emiliani; Josephine Bakhita; Cuthman
9 Apollonia; Miguel Febres Cordero
10 Clare of Rimini; Hugh of Fosses
11 Pascal; Theodora
12 Victoria; Benedict of Aniane; Eulalia of Barcelona
13 Jordan of Saxony; Christina of Spoleto
14 Cyril; Valentine
15 Georgia; Claude La Colombeère
16 Elias; Philippa Mareri; Nicholas Paglia
17 Theodore Tiro; Anne Wang; Finan of Lindisfarne
18 Colman of Lindisfarne; Gertrude Comensoli
19 Elizabeth Bartholomea Picenardi; Conrad of Piacenza
20 Leo of Catania; Thomas Pormont
21 Peter Damian; Robert Southwell; Noel Pinot
22 Isabel of France; Margaret of Cortona
23 Raphaela Ybarra de Villalonga; Antoninus
24 Mark dei Marconi; Josepha Naval Girbés; Robert of Arbrissel
25 Francisca-Ana Cirer Carbonell; Aloysius Versaglia
26 Victor the Hermit
27 Anne Line; Gabriel Possenti
28 Antonia of Florence; Daniel Brottier

March

1 David of Wales; Joanna Maria Bonomo
2 Angela of the Cross; Chad
3 Katharine Drexel; Samuel Marzorati
4 Alexander Blake; Nicholas Horner
5 Ciaran (Kieran) of Saighir
6 Agnes of Bohemia; Colette of Corbie
7 Perpetua; Felicity; John Baptist Nam Chong-Sam
8 John of God; Felix of Dunwich
9 Frances of Rome; Catherine of Bologna; Dominic Savio
10 Marie-Eugénie Milleret; John Ogilvie
11 Mark Chong Lu-bai; Alexius Ou Syei-Yeng
12 Symeon the New Theologian; Joseph Tchang Ta-Pong
13 Jeanne Véron
14 Matilda; James Cusmano
15 Zachary, pope; Louise de Marillac; Clement Mary Hofbauer
16 Robert Dalby
17 Patrick; Gertrude of Nivelles
18 Martha Le Bouteiller; Cyril; Edward
19 Joseph, the husband of Mary
20 Martin of Braga; Francis Palau y Quer
21 Benedicta Frassinello; Matthew Flathers
22 Nicholas of Flüe; Paul of Narbonne
23 Rebecca Al Rayes; Edmund Sykes
24 Catherine of Vadstena; Diego Joseph
25 James Bird; Margaret Clitherow; Lucy Filippini
26 Peter of Sebaste
27 Rupert of Salzberg; John the Egyptian
28 Renée-Marie Feillatreau; Christopher Wharton
29 Jonas; Gwladys (Gladys)
30 Peter Regaldo; Leonard Murialdo
31 Guy of Pomposa; Stephen of Mar Saba

April

1 Irene; Mary of Egypt; Valery (Walaricus); Hugh of Grenoble
2 Francis of Paola; Theodosia
3 Richard of Chichester

4 Benedict the Moor; Peter of Poitiers
5 Gerald of Sauve-Majeure; Eva of Liège; Juliana of Mount Cornillon
6 Willian of Eskill; Catherine of Pallanza
7 Ralph Ashley; Dominic Iturrate Zubero; John Baptist de la Salle
8 Julie Billiart; Walter of Pontoise
9 Thomas of Tolentino
10 Anthony Neyrot; Magdalen of Canossa
11 Gemma Galgani; Stanislaus of Cracow
12 Julius I, pope; Teresa of Los Andes
13 Martin I, pope; Ida of Boulogne; Margaret of Metola
14 Valerius; Bernard of Tiron
15 Damien De Veuster; Caesar de Bus
16 Bernadette; Joachim of Siena; Magnus of Orkney
17 Kateri Tekakwitha; Clare of Pisa; Robert of Chaise-Dieu
18 Alexander of Alexandria; Savina Petrilli
19 Leo IX, pope; James Duckett; Conrad of Parzham
20 Agnes of Montepulciano; Simon of Todi
21 Bartholomew of Cervere; Anselm
22 Theodore of Sykeon; Francis of Fabriano
23 George; Helen of Udine
24 Mary Euphrasia Pelletier; Benedict Menni
25 Mark; Franca of Piacenza
26 Stephen of Perm
27 Zita; Simeon of Jerusalem
28 Gianna Beretta Molla; Louis Marie Grignion; Peter Chanel; Cyril of Turov
29 Robert of Molesme; Catherine of Siena; Hugh of Cluny
30 Miles Gerard; Marie Guyart; Pauline Von Mallinckrodt

May

1 Joseph, the worker
2 Zoe; Anthony of Florence; Daniel of Syria; Boris of Bulgaria
3 Philip and James the Less; Maura; Emilia
4 Antonina; Gregory of Verucchio
5 Hilary of Arles; Angelo
6 Mary-Catherine of Cairo; Bartholomew of Montepulciano

7 Flavia Domitilla; Giselle of Bavaria; Rose Venerini; John of Beverley
8 Victor the Moor; Benedict II, pope
9 Thomas Pickering; Mary-Teresa Gerhardinger
10 Beatrice d'Este; Nicholas Albergati
11 Walter of L'Esterp; Francis de Girolamo; Matthew Le Van Gam
12 Imelda Lambertini; Dominic of the Causeway; Jane of Portugal
13 Andrew Fournet; Madeleine Albrici; Mel
14 Matthias; Mary Mazzarello; Michael Garicoïts
15 Rupert of Bingen; Isaiah of Rostov
16 Brendan of Clonfert; Simon Stock; Alexander of Caesarea
17 Antonia Mesina; Pascal Baylon; Peter Lieou
18 Blandina Merten; Eric of Sweden; Felix of Cantalice
19 Dunstan of Canterbury; Ivo of Brittany; Crispin of Viterbo
20 Columba of Rieti; Aurea of Ostia; Bernardine of Siena
21 Charles de Mazenod; Timothy the Deacon
22 Julia of Corsica; Rita of Cascia
23 William of Rochester; John Baptist Rossi
24 Agatha Kim; David of Scotland; Vincent of Lérins
25 Bede the Venerable; Madeleine Sophie Barat; Mary Magdalen of Pazzi
26 Mariana of Quito; Philip Neri
27 Julius the Veteran; Barbara Yi; Edmund Duke; Martha Kim
28 Bernard of Montjoux; Margaret Pole; William of Gellone
29 Bona of Pisa; Ursula Ledóchowska; Gerard of Burgundy
30 Joan of Arc; Basil and Emmelia; Luke Kirby
31 Noe Mawaggali; Petronilla

June
1 Justin Martyr; Simeon of Syracuse
2 Blandina; Marcellinus and Peter
3 Charles Lwanga; Kevin
4 Francis Caracciolo
5 Boniface; Ferdinand of Portugal
6 Philip the Deacon; Claude of Besançon
7 Baptista Varani; Robert of Newminster; Colman of Dromore
8 Melania the Elder; William of York
9 Diana d'Andalo; Columba of Iona; Silvester of Valdiseve

10 Henry of Treviso; Bonaventure Baduario
11 Paula Frassinetti; Mary Rose Molas y Vallvé; Barnabas
12 Antonina; John of Sahagún
13 Anthony of Padua; Gerard of Clairvaux
14 Methodius of Constantinople
15 Alice (Aleydis); Germaine of Pibrac
16 Julitta; Aurelian; Guy of Cortona
17 Hervé (Harvey); Peter of Pisa
18 Gregory Barbarigo
19 Juliana Falconieri; Bruno Querfurt; Thomas Woodhouse
20 Alban
21 Aloysius Gonzaga; Ralph of Bourges
22 John Fisher; Thomas More; Paulinus of Nola
23 Audrey (Etheldreda); Joseph Cafasso
24 John the Baptist
25 Prosper of Aquitaine; Maximus of Turin
26 John and Paul of Rome
27 Louisa de Montaignac; Cyril of Alexandria; George
   Mtasmindeli
28 John of Southworth
29 Peter; Paul; Judith; Emma; Raymond Lull
30 Martial of Limoges; Bertrand of Le Mans

July
1 Oliver Plunkett; Simeon Salas
2 Peter of Luxembourg
3 Thomas; Raymond of Toulouse
4 Elizabeth of Portugal; Bertha of Blangy; Andrew of Crete
5 Antony Zaccaria; Humphrey Pritchard
6 Maria Goretti; Mary Teresa Ledóchowska
7 Felix of Nantes; Roger Dickenson
8 Aquila and Prisca
9 Joan of Reggio; Pauline of the Sacred Heart
10 Cnut; Victoria and Anatolia
11 Benedict; Olga
12 Veronica; Leo of La Cava; John Jones
13 Silas; Mildred; Henry II, king
14 Vincent Madelgarius; Francis Solano

15 Edith of Polesworth; Vladimir of Kiev; Anne Mary Javouhey
16 Mary Magdalen Postel
17 Leo IV, pope; Marcellina; Justa and Rufina
18 Frederick of Utrecht; Bruno of Segni; Arnulf (Arnold) of Metz
19 Macrina the Younger; John Plessington
20 Joseph Díaz Sanjurjo
21 Angelina of Marsciano; Lawrence of Brindisi; Victor of
   Marseilles
22 Madeleine (Mary Magdalene); Augustine of Biella
23 Bridget of Sweden; John Cassian
24 Felicia of Milan; Nicholas Garlick; Louisa of Savoy
25 James the Greater; Christopher; Valentina
26 Joachim and Anne; Bartolomea Capitanio
27 Natalia and Aurelius; Clement of Ohrid
28 Victor, pope; Samson of Dol; Alphonsa Muttathupadathu
29 Martha, Mary, and Lazarus of Bethany
30 Peter Chrysologus; Julitta; Leopold Mandic
31 Helen of Skövde; Justin de Jacobis

August
1 Dominic Nguyen Van Hanh; Tomothy of the Hellespont
2 Joan of Aza; Stephen I, pope; Walter
3 Lydia; Martin of Campania
4 John Baptist Vianney; Cecilia Cesarini; Amata
5 Margaret the Barefooted; Oswald; Abel of Reims
6 Octavain of Savona; Justus
7 Afra; Albert of Trapani; Conrad Nantwein
8 Dominic; Mary MacKillop; Paul Keye-T'ing Chou
9 Teresa Benedicta of the Cross (Edith Stein); Richard Bere
10 Lawrence; Augustine Ota; Hugh of Auxerre
11 Clare of Assisi; Susanna; Alexander "the Charcoal-Burner"
12 Michael Nguyen Huy Ay; Lelia
13 Gertrude of Altenberg; William Freeman
14 Maximilian Kolbe; Elizabeth Renzi
15 Mary, the Mother of God; Stanislaus Kostka; Juliana Puricelli
16 Stephen of Hungary; Rock; Beatrice da Silva
17 Benedicta of Susteren; Luke Kiyemon
18 Helen; Leonard of Campania; Paula of Montaldo

19 Emily of Vercelli; John Eudes; Ezekiel Moreno Diaz
20 Bernard of Clairvaux; Rosa Kim; Lucy Kim
21 Victoria Rasoamanarivo; Joseph Dang Dinh Vièn
22 Sigfrid of Wearmouth; Timothy of Rome
23 Rose of Lima; Owen (Eugene)
24 Bartholomew; Emily de Vialar; Joan Antide-Thouret
25 Louis of France; Gregory of Utrecht
26 Elizabeth Bichier des Ages; Natalia and Adrian of Nicomedia
27 Monica; Roger Cadwallador; David Lewis
28 Augustine; Moses the Black; Edmund Arrowsmith
29 John the Baptist; Sabina
30 Margaret Ward; Edward Shelley
31 Joseph of Arimathea; Nicodemus; Raymond Nonnatus

September
1 Verena; Simeon Stylites the Elder; Giles; Lucy de Monte
2 William of Roskilde; Margaret of Louvain
3 Gregory the Great; Phoebe
4 Valerian; Ida of Herzfeld; Rosalia; Catherine of Racconigi
5 Bertinus; Gentilis
6 Magnus of Füssen; Stephen of Châtillon; Bertrand of Garrigues; Peregrin of Falarone
7 Regina; John of Nicomedia; Mark Körösi; Ralph Corby
8 Peter Claver; Seraphina Sforza
9 Isaac I, Katholikos of the Armenians; Kieran of Clonmacnois; Louisa of Savoy
10 Finnian of Moville; Nicholas of Tolentino; Ambrose Barlow
11 Theodora of Alexandria; Regula; Felix
12 Guy of Anderlecht; Francis of Calderola
13 Mary of Jesus; John Chrysostom
14 Albert of Jerusalem; Gabriel Taurin Dufresse
15 Catherine of Genoa; Ludmila; Roland de' Medici
16 Cyprian of Carthage; Euphemia; Ninian; Edith of Wilton; Victor III, pope; Louis Allemand
17 Hildegard of Bingen; Robert Bellarmine
18 Joseph of Cupertino; Lambert of Freising
19 Emily de Rodat; David of Yaroslavl
20 Francis de Posadas

21 Matthew; Maura of Troyes; Yu So-sa Cecilia; Nam I-gwan Sebastian
22 Maurice; Thomas of Villanova
23 Helen of Bologna; Linus
24 Gerard of Csanad; William Spenser
25 Herman the Cripple; Sergius of Radonezh; Finnbarr; Vincent Strambi
26 Lucy of Caltagirone; Theresa Couderc; Cosmas and Damian
27 Vincent de Paul; Mark Criado
28 Lioba; Wenceslas of Bohemia
29 Michael; Gabriel; Raphael
30 Jerome; Simon of Crépy; Frederick Albert

October

1 Thérèse of Lisieux; Romanus the Melodist
2 Anthony Chevrier
3 Thomas of Hereford; Gerard of Brogne
4 Francis of Assisi
5 Flora of Beaulieu; Bartholomew Longo
6 Faith; Bruno; Mary-Rose Durocher
7 Justina
8 Pelagia; Keyne
9 Denis; John Leonardi; Gunther; Louis Bertrán
10 Paulinus of York; Francis Borgia
11 Kenneth (Canice); Bruno the Great; Alexander Sauli; Mary Soledad
12 Wilfrid; Edwin; Maximilian of Lorch
13 Edward the Confessor; Gerald of Aurillac; Magdalen Panattieri; Daniel
14 Justus of Lyons
15 Teresa of Avila; Thecla of Kitzengen; Richard Gwyn
16 Hedwig; Margaret Mary Alacoque; Gerard Majella
17 Laurentine Prin; Ursula Bourla; Louise Ducrez
18 Luke
19 John de Brebeuf; Charles Garnier; Isaac Jogues; Gabriel Lalemant; Paul of the Cross
20 Andrew of Crete; Mary Bertilla Boscardin
21 John of Bridlington; James Strzemie

22 Philip of Heraclea

23 John of Capistrano; Ignatius of Constantinople; Arnold Rèche

24 Anthony Mary Claret; Joseph Baldo

25 Crispin; Christopher of Romagna; Thaddeus MacCarthy

26 Damian of Finale Borgo

27 Contardo Ferrini

28 Simon; Jude

29 Colman of Kilmacduagh; Abraham of Rostov

30 Benvenuta of Cividale; Angelo of Acri; Alphonsus Rodríguez

31 Quentin; Bee (Begu)

November

1 Mary of Rome; Rupert Mayer

2 Margaret of Lorraine; Thomas of Walden

3 Winifred; Martin de Porres; Ida of Fischingen; Malachy; Hubert

4 Frances of Amboise; Charles Borromeo

5 Zachary (Zechariah) and Elizabeth

6 Christina of Stommeln; Joan de Maillé; Leonard of Noblac

7 Anthony Baldinucci; Helen of Arcella; Margaret Colonna; Vincent Grossi

8 John Duns Scotus; Jeffrey (Godfrey) of Amiens; Elizabeth of the Trinity

9 Gratia of Cattaro; Louis Morbioli; George Napper

10 Leo the Great; Andrew Avellino

11 Martin of Tours; Bartholomew of Grottaferrata

12 Josaphat; Benedict of Kazimierz; Gabriel of Ancona

13 Brice; Kilian of Aubigny; Augustina Pietrantoni

14 Lawrence O'Toole

15 Albert the Great; Raphael Kalinowski

16 Margaret of Scotland; Gertrude the Great; Edmund of Abingdon

17 Elizabeth of Hungary; Hilda of Whitby; Hugh of Lincoln; Victoria

18 Philippine Duchesne; Caroline Kozka; Odo of Cluny

19 Salvator Lilli

20 Edmund; Mary Fortunata Viti

21 Mary Siedliska; Albert of Louvain
22 Cecilia; Arthur Bell
23 Clement of Rome; Michael Pro
24 Flora and Mary
25 Moses of Rome
26 Peter of Alexandria; Conrad of Constance; Delphina de Glandèves
27 Bernardino of Fossa; Virgil of Salzburg
28 Catherine Labouré; Stephen the Younger; James of the March
29 William Gibson; Francis of Lucera
30 Andrew; Cuthbert Mayne; Frederick of Regensburg; Alexander Crow

December

1 Edmund Campion; Ralph Sherwin; Hugh Faringdon
2 Mary Angela Astorch; Raphael Chylinsky
3 Francis Xavier; Edward Coleman
4 Fare; Osmund; Peter of Siena; Adolph Kolping
5 Crispina; Justinian; Christina of Markyate
6 Nicholas; Dionysia; Abraham of Kratia
7 Ambrose of Milan; Josepha Rossello
8 Mary, the Mother of God
9 Bernard Silvestrelli; Leocadia; Peter Fourier
10 Gregory III, pope; Jerome Ranuzzi
11 Daniel the Stylite; Damasus I, pope; Melchior Sánchez
12 Jane Frances de Chantal; Finnian of Clonard; Simon Hoa
13 Lucy; Odilia; Anthony Grassi
14 John of the Cross; Frances Schervier; Bonaventure Buonaccorsi
15 Maria di Rosa; Valerian; Virginia Centurione-Bracelli
16 Adelaide of Burgundy; Clement Marchisio
17 Begga; Joseph Manyanet y Vivès
18 Flannan of Killaloe; Paul My; Rufus
19 Stephen Vinh; Urban V, pope
20 Ammon; Dominic of Siloa
21 Peter Canisius; Peter Thi
22 Frances Xavier Cabrini; Adam of Loccum
23 Margaret of Savoy; Hartmann

24 Irmina; Adela; Paula Cerioli

25 Anastasia; Eugenia; Albert Chmielkowski

26 Stephen; Agnes Phila; Vicentia López y Vicuña

27 John; Fabiola

28 Matthia of Matelica; Theodore the Sanctified

29 Thomas à Becket; Marcellus Akimetes

30 Sebastian of Esztergom; Edgwin

31 Melania the Younger; Sylvester I, pope; Columba of Sens